I0797788

POUTINE NATION

SYLVAIN CHARLEBOIS

POUTINE NATION

LESSONS FROM THE UNGLAMOROUS RISE OF A CANADIAN CULINARY ICON

AEVO UNIVERSITY OF TORONTO PRESS

Aevo UTP
An imprint of the University of Toronto Press
Toronto Buffalo London
utppublishing.com

ISBN 978-1-4875-4161-3 (cloth)
ISBN 978-1-4875-4178-1 (EPUB)
ISBN 978-1-4875-4164-4 (PDF)

Library and Archives Canada Cataloguing in Publication

Title: Poutine nation : lessons from the unglamorous rise of a Canadian culinary icon / Sylvain Charlebois.
Names: Charlebois, Sylvain, author.
Description: Includes bibliographical references and index.
Identifiers: Canadiana (print) 20250252732 | Canadiana (ebook) 20250252961 | ISBN 9781487541613 (hardcover) | ISBN 9781487541781 (EPUB) | ISBN 9781487541644 (PDF)
Subjects: LCSH: Poutine—Social aspects—Québec (Province) | LCSH: Poutine—Social aspects—Canada. | LCSH: Poutine—Economic aspects—Québec (Province) | LCSH: Poutine—Economic aspects—Canada. | LCSH: Cooking, French-Canadian. | LCSH: National characteristics, Canadian.
Classification: LCC TX803.P8 C43 2025 | DDC 641.82—dc23

Printed in Canada

Cover design: Kristjan Buckingham
Cover image: iStock.com/Planet Flem

We wish to acknowledge the land on which the University of Toronto Press operates. This land is the traditional territory of the Wendat, the Anishnaabeg, the Haudenosaunee, the Métis, and the Mississaugas of the Credit First Nation.

University of Toronto Press acknowledges the financial support of the Government of Canada, the Canada Council for the Arts, and the Ontario Arts Council, an agency of the Government of Ontario, for its publishing activities.

Canada Council for the Arts
Conseil des Arts du Canada

Funded by the Government of Canada
Financé par le gouvernement du Canada

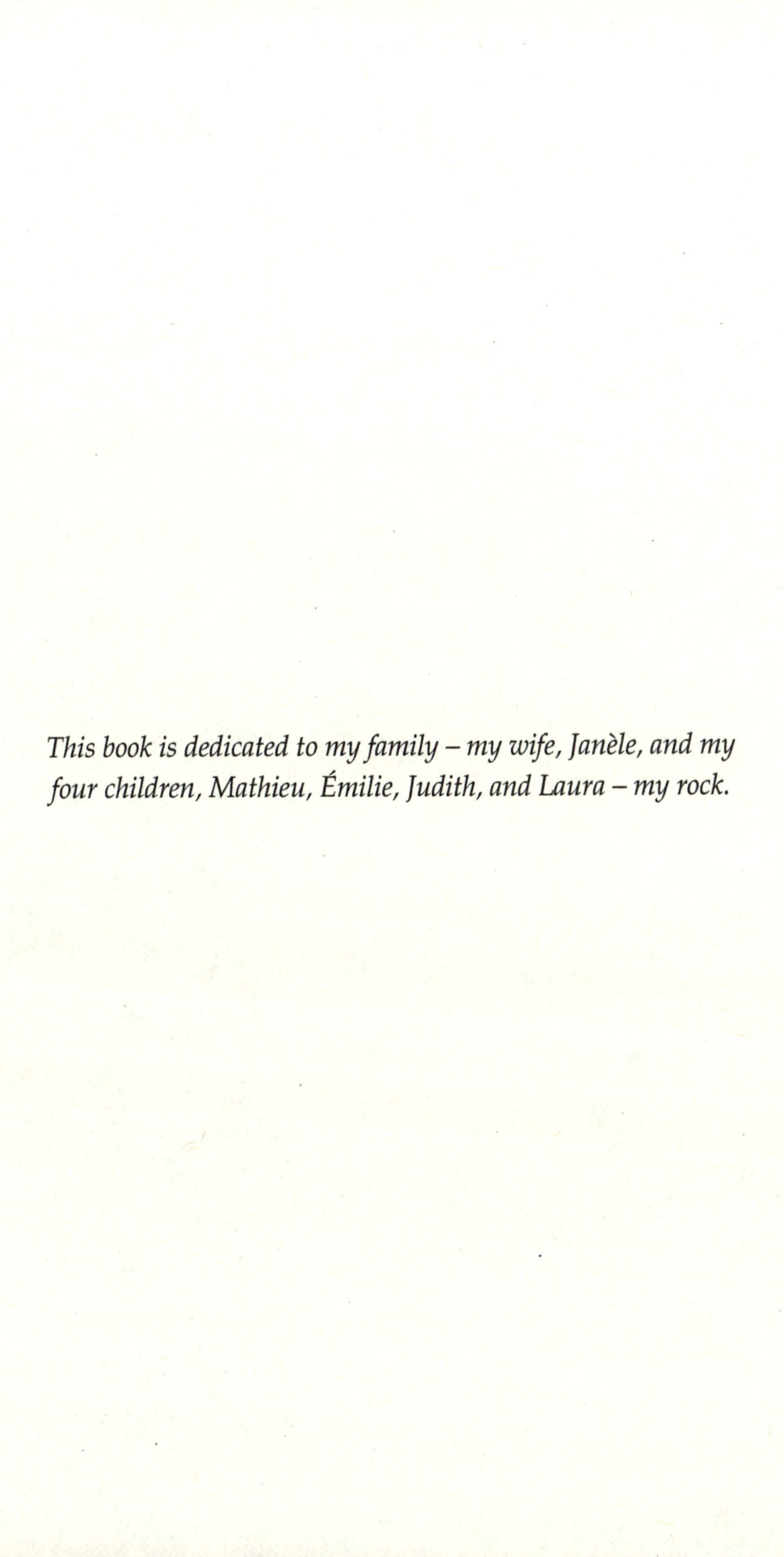

This book is dedicated to my family – my wife, Janèle, and my four children, Mathieu, Émilie, Judith, and Laura – my rock.

Contents

Photos

Preface

This book is not necessarily about poutine, but more so about how a dish, as crude as poutine is, has risen to international fame. Before writing this book, I could not understand the appeal and love of poutine as I have never craved the dish. However, I appreciate and believe that poutine is something special.

While I've had the pleasure of writing several books before this one, this one holds personal meaning for me – not to mention how this has been the most enjoyable book I've written. I wrote this book to honour my family, my hometown of Farnham, and my home province of Quebec. Writing this book was a personal journey for me as I wanted to understand how a simple, unhealthy dish has become a Canadian icon. While Canadians appear to be polite and reserved, we do take a great amount of pride in things that are truly Canadian. We take pride in things that represent us as Canadians: the beaver, the maple leaf, maple syrup, the mounted police, hockey, and now poutine.

This is not the first book written about poutine, but I believe it is the first book written in English that also includes a global perspective on the iconic dish. One of the best books I have read about poutine is *Maudite Poutine!* [*Damned Poutine!*] by Charles-Alexandre Théorêt. It was the most honest, humble book looking at poutine. After reading Théorêt's book I wanted to build on his work and to assess how poutine has become an international success. I also wanted to study what we can learn from the dish's journey over the years. Anne Hui's *Chop Suey Nation* also inspired me to write this book. Hui's idea of travelling across the country and visiting small-town Chinese restaurants to honour her roots motivated me to do the same for poutine.

Finally, I would be remiss if I did not thank my family, who were there when I first tasted poutine when growing up in Farnham. I'd like to thank my father, Michel, and my mother, Lyse Lafrance-Charlebois, who passed away in 2009, my older brother Jean-René and my twin brother Patrick, my extended family, particularly Diane (Tantine), Michel, Richard, Pierrette, and friends who were there when I was trying to figure out my place in life. Today, I'm supported by my loving family: my wife, Janèle, and my children, Mathieu, Émilie, Judith, and Laura. The family members on my wife's side, the Préfontaines and the Vezeaus, are always a joy to visit and spend time with: Jean-Marc, my father-in-law, his lovely partner, Johann, and my mother-in law, Nicole, who passed away in 2018. I am truly blessed to have all of these great people in my life. As for my four children, I can assure you that they all have had poutine, in and outside of Quebec. They all have their opinions on whose poutine is best, but that I won't disclose.

I want to assure readers, especially my environmentalist and fiscally conservative friends, that this project was self-funded and almost carbon-neutral. During my poutine pilgrimage, I only ate poutine in cities that I was visiting for business or for conferences (except for my trip to Australia). I paid for my own poutines and taxis, used my own car, and wrote the bulk of this book between 3 a.m. and 7 a.m., so that this project wouldn't interfere with my duties as a father and as an academic. This book is not just about poutine, but rather it is about our relationship with food and how a phenomenon like poutine can happen. I also wanted to make sure taxpayers were not paying for what I considered to be a special, personal journey.

Introduction

This book is about *the* poutine, the controversial, unhealthy, but miraculously well-known dish you can find all around the world. For most of us, poutine is now an iconic dish. But this transformation has occurred over just a few decades.

The subject of this book, the poutine we know in Canada and now around the world, is made of fries, cheese curds, and gravy. Poutine has accomplished much since its creation in 1957. Indeed, its three simple ingredients were all that was needed to brand our nation or food culture, such that many people associate Canada with poutine.

In its simplicity, poutine has an intriguing story. According to archives, poutine's birthplace is in the province of Quebec, in a rural region called les Bois-Francs, or Centre-du-Québec.[1] Some reports suggest poutine was first served in 1957.[2] A few locations claim to be its birthplace, notably Drummondville, Warwick, Plessisville, Victoriaville, Matane, Saguenay, and Princeville, among other places. While writing this book, I have received several reports from individuals claiming that they were the true poutine inventor, with no authoritative evidence. Some communities in Acadia also claim to be the birthplace of a different version of poutine, such as the Acadian poutine. However, no one is truly certain about its creation.

The first intention of this book was to try to definitively determine who created poutine, searching for its origins objectively and with unprejudiced clarity. Second, I wanted to investigate how it became an iconic dish. At the outset, all that I knew for sure was that poutine was created in a town not too far from my birthplace, Farnham, Quebec, in the Eastern Townships.[3]

Poutine Nation is a tale of three stories. It is a story of poutine, the story of my home province, Quebec, and the story of my life where poutine made an impact. It is difficult to separate these three threads. During my research, I came to realize why poutine was created and why it had to be produced in my home province, in my region. Growing up in Farnham, I had no idea that poutine "happened" a few kilometres away from me. I thought everyone everywhere knew what poutine was.

I can safely say that when you look at the dish's legacy over the years, poutine is a miracle of Canadian gastronomy. It became renowned despite its obvious flaws. The average male needs to run 150 minutes in order to burn the 1,400 calories of a typical poutine.[4] Doctors warn us against consuming that amount of fat and sodium in a standard serving. Indeed, eating poutine once a day, every day, would alarm your doctors; it would be a death sentence.

Poutine was originally a dish served in rural communities by small canteens or little restaurants on the main street of small towns in Quebec. At first sight, poutine is not an attractive dish. Cakes, pastries, sushi, even spaghetti or a roast are appealing to the eye, whereas poutine looks like a soupy, cheesy mush. Nevertheless, it has gained prominence over the last three decades and is now served in thousands of restaurants and in thousands of versions around the world.[5] Franchises like Smoke's Poutinerie lead its international promotion, and it can even be found at major chains such as McDonald's, Wendy's, KFC, and Burger King.[6]

Other iconic Canadian dishes such as the Nanaimo bar, split pea soup, tourtière, the BeaverTail, and the butter tart have been influenced by foreign food culture and partially created abroad.[7] Poutine, however, was created in Canada, with no influence from other parts of the world. What is interesting about poutine is its capacity to adapt and change. Similar to pizza or the hamburger, poutine adapts to different tastes and trends and can expand its market by adding unique ingredients. Once considered an affordable, humble dish, it is now served at some restaurants with lamb, lobster, foie gras, gold flakes, and other expensive ingredients.[8] Once a snack, it is now served as breakfast, lunch, dinner, a side dish, an appetizer, or even as a dessert. Poutine is literally everywhere and is offered in many different forms.

The commonness of its ingredients makes it accessible for the entire world, as long as you are not fussy about curds or a specific gravy. First, potatoes are one of the most common crops in the world. They can even grow in space.[9] Second, cheese is also a popular item in the industrialized world.

Produced in different forms, cheese is available almost everywhere.[10] Finally, gravy helps poutine to please any palate. Easy access to ingredients makes the dish less foreign and easier to prepare, helping it gain worldwide fame.

The name "poutine" is also captivating. For non-French-speaking people, the word can be difficult to pronounce.[11] Yet, when travelling around the world, restaurants continue to call it poutine. Few have been tempted to change the name or to call it something else. And like most fast-food dishes, its origins have been debated for many years. This book looks at poutine's history and attempts to clarify key moments and people who have made a difference, asking: Is poutine Canadian? French Canadian? Or Québécois? Outside Canada, few people know that poutine came from Quebec. Should we care? As a Quebecer, I know that many others do.

While there are reasons why we should not care whether the world knows that poutine is from Quebec, there is, however, one reason that is worth mentioning. Unlike many other food trends throughout history, poutine did not originate in a major urban centre. Most fast-food inventions, even culinary creations and trends, have started in cities. Poutine, on the other hand, was created in the countryside in one of two small towns: Warwick or Drummondville. Warwick's population today is barely five thousand. Drummondville's population is larger, with roughly seventy-five thousand. Nevertheless, compared to Napoli (famous for the classic Neapolitan pasta dishes) or Hamburg (fish dishes and the hamburger), these places are quite small. And yet, a few tales and a simple mixture of three ingredients have caught the imagination of millions. When I grew up, Farnham had five thousand people, so I can certainly relate to the pride that small towns feel when thinking about poutine and its popularity. *Poutine Nation* explores this dimension of the famous dish as well.

Poutine is now almost as well-known as other fast-food staples such as hot dogs, hamburgers, and pizzas. It is a financially accessible, arena-friendly dish served at most hockey rinks, food trucks, fast-food joints, and snack bars in the country. Many Canadians believe poutine to be one of the country's best creations. It has made the top ten of Canada's most significant culinary contributions and has often been ranked number one.[12] Despite its success, it hasn't been a source of pride for Quebecers. In fact, poutine has been viewed in Quebec as a dish created as an afterthought and a butt of jokes. Chefs and restaurateurs snubbed the dish for several years. Despite its market success, the word "poutine" was not added to the Merriam-Webster dictionary until 2014.[13] Yet today, many eateries add poutine to their menus to create an attractive portfolio of familiar and enticing junk food.

Poutine Nation dissects the dish's journey to stardom, starting with its unassuming beginnings in rural Quebec and its leap onto the international stage. This book also looks at many aspects of food trends and our relationship with food. Most importantly, *Poutine Nation* sets the stage for how poutine fits in our food universe. Through personal anecdotes and research, *Poutine Nation* will dig into the dish's quirky past and explain its fascinating resilience over the years. As such, *Poutine Nation* takes us around the world and looks at the stories of poutine pioneers and the people who made the dish well-known around the world. *Poutine*

Nation is not only about how a dish becomes a cultural icon, but also how it is an ambassador to a culture.

This book is not solely about the dish itself; rather, it is more about people, food cultures, and the economics and politics of food. *Poutine Nation* looks at a variety of issues affecting our relationship with food, the politics behind the dish itself, and how it has been used in the past. Poutine has been referenced in many political campaigns in Quebec. Many Canadians would remember the infamous robocall scandal that occurred during a federal election campaign in 2011, intended to suppress voting.[14] The robocalls came from a burner phone registered to a fictional "Pierre Poutine."[15]

Essentially, *Poutine Nation* looks at how a simple recipe took the world by storm despite its imperfection. Some argue that the word "poutine" means "a mess," but it's not clear how the name is connected to such a meaning. Is poutine a mess, literally and physically? This book's underlying goal is to truly understand what poutine means to Quebec, to Canada, to Canadians, and to a food culture looking to make a worthwhile contribution within its borders as well as internationally.

As I mentioned, many books have been written in French about Quebec's culinary traditions and poutine, such as Théorêt's excellent *Maudite Poutine!*[16] However, as a Quebecer, I wanted to share my province's unique story with English-speaking Canada and the rest of the world through poutine's journey, complementing all the work written in French on poutine.

Poutine's success has created a malaise among gastronomic elites and in culinary spheres. Nonetheless, poutine owes its success to something more profound, something that goes beyond trends. Poutine has become a dish for the common people, a democratic expression of what food is to a population, a powerful gastronomic symbol with many meanings. *Poutine Nation* discovers how poutine's triumph as a global dish is multi-faceted.

I had a lot of fun writing this book. It was the easiest thing I've ever had to do since I began my academic career. Unlike the academic papers I write, this book is about understanding humans and how food affects us. The time I spent writing it has helped me to understand how humans define themselves through food. A culinary icon causes people to think about history, where we have come from, and how we interact as social beings. Poutine's story is very much about how we form a society through food.

Poutine Nation is not intended to debate taste, discuss how to make the best poutine, or share who serves the best poutine. Tastes are arbitrary, and everyone is entitled to their opinion. Food is personal, and with Quebecers, poutine can get *very* personal. It would have been challenging to define a great poutine, especially as it has been recreated, revised, and enjoyed around the world. Some Quebecers get upset when they see versions like hot pot pie poutine, pizza poutine, or eggs Benedict poutine. It is shocking, but it is the price of poutine's global socialization.

This book is very much about celebrating poutine's global success as a Canadian iconic dish. Its rise to fame is nothing short of unpredictably spectacular.

All that said, everyone knows that the best poutine in the world is in Farnham, Quebec, at L'Ami du Passant. Just saying.

PART I

First Times

CHAPTER ONE

My First Taste of Poutine: Farnham, Quebec

Farnham is in the Eastern Townships, about an hour southeast of Montreal. It was known for its railways, army camp, carpet industry, and farms. Farnham did have some textile plants, but the majority had closed before I was born. When I was growing up, Farnham felt far away from Montreal. But with time, Montreal's urban sprawl got closer to Farnham, or perhaps it was the other way around and Farnham got closer to Montreal. So, in time, staying in Farnham has developed its own appeal. Houses are cheaper, and living in the country is now sought after by hipsters. However, when I was living in Farnham, things were different.

When I was young, everyone wanted to leave Farnham after high school. There was little pride in living in a small rural town. I played for the local American football team, the Astérix, and my high school volleyball team. I felt more pride playing for sports teams than I did living in Farnham.

My feelings about Farnham have changed over time. My mother became the town's mayor for a decade (1991–2000), and my older brother, Jean-René, became a highly respected businessperson there. As I've grown older, I have acquired a better sense of the world and a new respect for my roots, my past, and my upbringing. My pride in coming from Farnham has only grown since I left. This may happen to people who come from small rural communities.

My classmates who stayed in Farnham after our graduation in 1987 were either farmers or content to stick around. I believed that if you wanted to change the world, you had to leave Farnham. Our high school was a decent-sized place with almost one thousand students, two hundred in our class. For my classmates, leaving was a liberation, a path to hope, to a better place, to a place where you could do something with your life. Those who left never returned, other than to visit. There have been a few school reunions, but nothing too fancy. Most of them were organized impromptu and not well attended. For many of us, Farnham was a place to forget. However, as I've grown older, I miss Farnham, the region, the memories, family, and friends.

I can't help but feel nostalgic about the town, about what I left behind. My parents' home on Main Street, the high school, parks where we spent time as lost souls growing up – I miss them all. I'll admit, going back has always been surprisingly nice. There is a park there named after my late mother, "Lyse Lafrance-Charlebois Park," located a few metres away from where she is buried.

I also miss the poutine; the one taste I cannot get anywhere else. I'm not sure if it is the location, the recipe, or the memories. But every time I go back to visit family and friends, I have to taste the poutine I grew up with. That connection has remained strong. It's hard to describe. Similar to other places in Canada, things continue to change in Farnham. Yet for the students after my graduating class, staying in Farnham after you were done high school has become trendy and accepted; it's okay to stick around. The one thing that hasn't changed is the poutine.

I can't exactly remember the first time I ate it. Ordering poutine was what you did, similar to just ordering fries at a french fry truck at the roadside. It's just what you did.

Like most good poutine places in rural Quebec, L'Ami Du Passant looked like a simple little old shack on Main Street, about a mile away from my house and a mile from the school. The place still looked the same until 2025 when it was demolished and rebuilt, almost exactly at the same location. But the new is almost like the old, with some changes.

The old place looked like any ordinary chip shack you would find in rural Quebec. There was no place to sit, just counters where you could stand to eat your poutine or whatever you ordered. There was room for no more than five to seven people inside. There was a booth on the side of Main Street where you ordered your food. Most people ordered out to eat at home, at work, or on a nearby park bench. There was one toilet, which always looked like it needed cleaning. The place looks almost dirty. However, I have never heard a comment about how the place looked, not once. In French, L'Ami du Passant means "friends of the passerby." And that's how it felt.

When I was growing up in Farnham, L'Ami du Passant was owned by a quiet man we knew as Émile. His actual name was Émilien Arbour. In fact, most people called the place "Chez Émile," or "Chez Ti-Mile," and not L'Ami du Passant. Few knew him personally, but everyone knew who he was. His restaurant sponsored local sports teams, and he always attended games. He was generous and committed to sports even though he was known to be the king of junk food. He was a bit of a legend in Farnham. He came to football games to watch us play, rain or shine. I'm sure most small towns in Quebec had someone like that. He worked long hours, every day for decades. He did not have a family or children, at least not that I know of. One or two of my friends worked there. It was such a small place that only two or three people could work there at a time. Emile was just a guy who worked late at night in his shack serving food to people in town, regulars or others passing through. He was open most days, working away almost to the time of his death in 1994. I don't think Émile really knew the role he played in the lives of many people like me, who were trying to figure things out as we grew up in a rural town.

Often after a sports tournament, we stopped at a restaurant and picked up a poutine. It made us forget the game if we had lost. The simple life. I assume kids today are still looking for that refuge at the same place I used to go. Despite smartphones and today's obsession with social media, it is nevertheless impossible to replicate what you get at L'Ami du Passant. Full stop. The place now has new owners. I don't know who they are. I also don't know most of the people who live in Farnham anymore. One thing is clear, though. The new owners have tried to keep everything the same. When I went back last year to Farnham, everything looked the same, except that the poutine is now offered with canard (duck) confit. That tells you how much the clientele has changed. When we were growing up, poutine was a meal, a snack, a treat, a reward after school, after a volleyball or a hockey tournament, a distraction to the pains of growing up in rural Quebec.

We did not know it then, but L'Ami du Passant was a portal to a much larger system, an industry called junk food. Everyone has memories of a place they went to for their junk-food fix. Canadians and Americans eat a lot of junk food every day, about 160 to 200 calories a day on average. Poutine arrived in the market at the same time as buffets and the supersizing phenomena. It was about providing more calories for less money. Eating for fuel and fun was king for the longest time. In those days, we did not question much of anything and just accepted things as they were. L'Ami du Passant operated in the age of fast-food innocence, and it worked. Today, food has been politicized, too much so in my mind. Writing a book on poutine could be seen by some as a gesture to encourage people to eat more junk food, which, of course, is nonsense. The important thing is to appreciate how things are the way they are. There is something about poutine that resonates in many of us, and writing a book on it is important.

Whether poutine is sold and served in a small shack like L'Ami du Passant or by a franchise around the world, poutine offers a different meaning to different people. That's not going to change.

CHAPTER TWO

Poutine?!

What can we learn from poutine's rise to fame? What does it say about our society? Why has poutine become so popular when other dishes, perhaps more refined and exquisite, are not as popular? This book is not just about poutine; it is also about how we socialize and democratize food over time.

I have been asked often why a "serious academic" would write a book on poutine. Well, to me, poutine is an excuse to write about food and where I'm from. I could not think of a better case study that looks at the history of Quebec and how a simple dish can be so successful. *Poutine Nation* relates Quebec's culture to the rest of the world while honouring my heritage, my past. I have also travelled enough to realize that poutine is something special, and its story needed to be written.

When I was growing up, I never questioned the name "poutine" or its meaning, either. Where I come from, most people don't. We eat junk food all the time without questioning what a hot dog, a hamburger, or pizza mean. Some people have argued that poutine means "mess" in French. It doesn't really, but it does suggest "putting in" something different, such as cheese with fries, or mixing ingredients that you normally wouldn't. It is when I started to travel and live outside of Quebec that I found myself being asked what "poutine" meant as a word. I had no idea and felt like I was disconnected from my heritage. It's something I should have known.

What I do remember is how difficult it was to get a poutine outside of Quebec. In 1987, I enrolled in the military as an air force officer. I was seventeen, and I left home clueless about the world. It was close to impossible to get a poutine, and I missed it. The only place you could get a poutine in those days was the officer's mess when we celebrated St-Jean-Batiste Day, on June 24, or else at some shady-looking junk-food joint near the base. These shacks were not easy to find. As I arrived on base in Shearwater, BC, for the first time, I saw a sign outside a small restaurant reading, "Poutine Here." I didn't know much about Canada as a whole then, but seeing the word "poutine" outside of Quebec made me feel welcomed as a French Canadian. I could tell that many people outside of Quebec didn't necessarily understand Quebec's culture, but that making us feel comfortable was important to them.

This is something many Quebecers don't appreciate but should. When leaving the province, Canadians are friendly and courteous, and they want to make us feel at ease despite what they may have heard.[1] I have seen it in Saskatchewan,

Guelph, Halifax, everywhere. Even when the separatist movement was at its height, Canadians focused on the person visiting from Quebec, not the politics. In a way, whenever I saw a place where poutine was sold, it felt like they wanted me, wanted us, to feel like we had never left Quebec. They knew leaving Quebec as a teenager was not easy – leaving any place is not easy, really. And every time we tried a poutine outside of Quebec, while it was not close to what we had back home, it did not matter. That moment when we were served a poutine outside the province, as young, foolish French Canadian officers, that's when we knew everything would be all right. To this day, I'm thankful for all these pioneers who opted to sell us poutine without questioning it. We were not judged. To me, that is a Canada that is often underappreciated. I was privileged to understand that early on in my life.

Today, poutine is everywhere. Unless you have been living under a rock, you know what poutine is.[2] Even the Quebec fast-food chain Valentine is petitioning for a poutine emoji. Within fifty years, poutine went from a side dish on a small-town restaurant's menu to a cultural culinary icon. From its humble beginnings, it is now a dish that captures the imagination of many, many people. Poutine has brought people together through companies, events, and festivals, not to mention how other cultures have adopted poutine by adding ingredients that are intricate parts of their cultural heritages. There are literally thousands of different versions of poutine now. It's impossible to generate a complete and accurate list of all varieties available.

Even IBM's question-answering computing system, Watson, got into it a few years ago.[3] IBM and the Institute of Culinary Education in New York City worked together, pushing Watson to go beyond answering Jeopardy questions and create new recipes. In one experiment, they prepared Watson's recipes for variations on poutine. Recipes such as Peruvian Potato Poutine, Viet-Thai Green Curry Poutine, and Haitian-Greek Veggie Poutine were developed. With artificial intelligence, computers came up with new recipes, reinventing poutine with innovative nuances.

Quite frankly, it's difficult to separate poutine's story from Canadian history as a young country, as a nation in the New World. Its affordability and simplicity make its socioeconomics so fascinating. When I travel around the world, poutine is arguably the first thing that comes up in a conversation about Canadian cuisine. Maple syrup does take its due place, as perhaps other dishes do, but poutine is now well-known, intertwined with our country's history and image.

Poutine may not be a stroke of culinary genius, but it has been around a long time. Its simple ingredients can be prepared in many different ways to adapt it to different tastes, different regions, and different styles. Believe it or not, it is also quite possible to make a healthier version of a poutine. The average-sized poutine contains well over a thousand calories, with many grams of fat and sodium. So, the incentive to make it healthier is certainly there.

Even though poutine is a simple dish, it remains at the centre of a peculiar mystery. How can such a simple, unhealthy dish become so well-known around the world? While there are books that have been dedicated to poutine, most are cookbooks or essays in French. Much of the work has been about the ingredients, recipes, and stories related to food and poutine. This book will dig much deeper into the history, determinants, and meaning of poutine's success for Quebec, Canada, and the rest of the world.

CHAPTER THREE

What Is Poutine, Really?

Food is often an intrinsic component of national identity and pride, but expressing what constitutes a Canadian cuisine has proven difficult due to the country's short culinary history and mix of immigrant cuisines. Poutine may not be a sophisticated dish, but it has nevertheless become a symbol associated with Canada. Yet the dish itself takes several forms – what actually constitutes poutine, this symbol of Canada or Quebec?

For most Quebecers a poutine has three key ingredients: cheese curds, french fries, and gravy. The earliest forms of poutine didn't include gravy, and some, like the original poutine lovers, don't enjoy the way gravy blends the ingredients together. Modern poutine, however, combines all three ingredients, if not more.[1] Yet, french fries, gravy, and cheese curds are essential ingredients to the definition of poutine. It's all about those three.

Most who have eaten poutine would agree that every bite is dynamic. Food scientists Robert J. Hyde and Steven A. Witherly argue that "most highly palatable foods are likely to have higher levels of dynamic contrast."[2] In other words, your mouth experiences different moments of taste and texture, making the experience unique. Dynamic contrast is typically experienced through texture contrasts of liquid/solid and soft/hard, but temperature, stickiness, and annoyance are also recognized as important factors. Cereal in milk, for instance, becomes an unappealing mush over time, while porridge is a boring meal for many because of the lack of contrast and dynamics. Conversely, poutine has many contrasting elements: the fries are crisp, the cheese squeaks then melts, and the gravy (or *sauce*, as we say in French) makes everything work together – or it can ruin everything. The gravy melds together the textures and flavours from the other two ingredients, and the incongruent ingredients become an amalgamated dish. Without the proper equipment and knowledge of the three ingredients, it is challenging to replicate the perfect mix at home. Even some restaurants can't do it well and hide their imperfections with extra ingredients.

Indeed, unlike most other types of junk food, most poutines are consumed in restaurants. Many people make their own hamburgers, hot dogs, and even pizzas at home. Poutine, however, is different. Rarely do people attempt to make poutine at home. Some do, but it's not the same. Perhaps it's because most people fail to replicate the unique taste of their favourite poutine at home, whether due to different recipes or kitchen equipment.

Cheese Curds and Their Squeakiness: The Butterfly of Cheese

The addition of cheese marks the beginning of poutine. Unlike fries, cheesemaking is complicated. There are so many different varieties and tastes. Most people can make fries and gravy at home, but cheese is a different matter. When making poutine, access to cheese, the right kind of cheese, is critical.[3] This is the one aspect of poutine exported outside Quebec that has attracted the most criticism. For many, cheese curds are the signature ingredient and must be added to the dish, the right way, at the right temperature. Few poutine lovers will forgive any anomalies when it comes to cheese and poutine. It's a sensitive issue, even for me.

The combination of cheese curds and fries was momentous, like chocolate and peanut butter – who can't resist a peanut butter cup? It was always meant to be, and a wonder it didn't happen before 1957. Fries served as cheese melts over them – what a stroke of genius!

Around the world, different kinds of cheese are used to make poutine. For people in Quebec, those who make poutine without cheese curds are amateurs. It's just not the same without the curds. But when you have a company like McDonald's pushing the product, supplies are an issue. There aren't enough producers to make enough cheese curds for the whole world. Substituting cheese curds with whatever cheese is available has become a common practice. Cheese curds are made mostly in Eastern Canada (Quebec, Ontario, New Brunswick, Nova Scotia) and in the

Eastern United States. The American cheese state is Wisconsin, and most Wisconsinites would know what cheese curds are. Cheesemaking is taken very seriously in Wisconsin. Curds have an entire festival to themselves every June in Ellsworth, Wisconsin. Its population is under four thousand people, but thousands venture to Ellsworth in June to celebrate cheese curds.

Quebecers won't call it poutine unless the dish has cheese curds. A poutine needs that squeaky sound that it makes when chewing curds. But to make that sound, the cheese has to be at room temperature, perhaps slightly warmer, when it comes into contact with the fries and gravy. Putting cheese curds in a fridge before serving is like putting a canoe upside down in the water. However, for food safety reasons, many do put the curds into the refrigerator, which causes them to lose their squeaky sound and become just ordinary cheese.

When I was young, I did not realize that this unique product was not well-known around the country. There is no official data, but some believe there to be over three hundred kinds of cheese curd. Most convenience stores and grocery stores in Eastern Canada sell cheese curds. Those who know about cheese curds outside Quebec often call it "squeaky cheese" and eat it as a snack, but the first time that most people taste cheese curds is when they eat their first poutine. For most, cheese curds equal poutine.

Cheese curds are salty, mild, and have the same density as normal cheese, but they feel rubbery between the teeth.[4] Cheese curds are often the freshest form of cheddar. In fact, cheese curds are fresh by-products of cheddar cheese, but some can be made from mozzarella, colby, or Monterey Jack. It should be noted that "Canadian legislation authorizes the retail sale of fresh Cheddar cheese curds made from pasteurized milk and kept at room temperature until 24 h after manufacturing. After that, the cheese curds must be stored at 4°C," for up to three days.[5] While most cheeses take roughly sixty days to coagulate, cheese curds are ready much sooner. Cheese curds are considered by cheesemakers to be a premature cheese.[6]

Suffice it to say, curds are a unique type of cheese, the butterflies of the cheese world: beautiful, transcendent, short-lived.[7] In addition to their squeakiness and short shelf life, they melt differently from most cheeses, behaving instead like the Greek cheese halloumi. The curds don't lose their shape when they become warmed by the fries and gravy – they soften. If curds need to travel a great deal, they often lose their squeaky sound and feel, which may explain why most cheese curds are not the same elsewhere when compared with Quebec's curds. Some poutine places use smaller cheese curds, about the size of peanuts, while Quebec's curds are as big as peanuts in their shells, creating a significant difference for the diner.

Cheese curds, like the other ingredients in a poutine, are high in calories. It takes a lot of dairy to produce them, about ten kilos of milk for one kilo of curds.[8] That is a little more than the average cheese, which may explain why cheese curds are more calorific. There are approximately 110 calories in one serving of cheese curds, and most of these calories (80!) come from fat. Worse, that includes 5.5 grams of saturated fat and enough sodium to make your heart bleed. So, despite creating a perfect harmony between the fries and the gravy, cheese curds are far from healthy, surprising no one.

Fries: Poutine's Bedrock

Poutine has achieved a form of social mobility beyond what we have seen with other Canadian dishes,[9] but it couldn't have done it without the mighty potato. Indeed, poutine even made its way onto the Canadian State Dinner menu organized by the White House in March 2016.[10]

Potatoes are everywhere yet underground, literally and figuratively, a part of the Canadian agriculture landscape for a long time. It is a vegetable, but mostly a source of starch, consumed as fries or chips. Potatoes have survived the test of time and have become a central part of our diet, whether young, old, poor, or rich, no matter where you are in the world.

I remember growing potatoes in our garden when I was young. We had rows and rows of potatoes in a garden almost half the size of a football field. To me, it seemed like it was the actual size of a football field. The potato is so easy to plant. We used to cut a potato into many pieces and put them into the ground. Months later, these pieces became plants. We also dug up the soil to encourage the growth of more potatoes. They were rewarding to cultivate but a lot of work. Nature at its best. In the winter, with three growing boys at home and a small budget, this source of starch was crucial. They weren't the healthiest source of nutrients, but they were filling and helped us, like many other families, get through the winter months.

The potato is the bedrock of poutine, the one ingredient that has made the dish easy to globalize. The whole world knows what a potato is. The potato plant always seemed to be fragile, often infected by pests, and we had to treat our plants almost every other week. It's not surprising that humanity has seen famines caused by potato crop losses, like the Irish famine of 1845.[11] During the famine, Ireland experienced a significant population decline as roughly one million died while another million people emigrated from the island. As a result, the total population dropped by nearly a quarter. Still, potatoes are resilient. With research, the crop has grown in popularity and adapted to various climates.[12]

The potato has been cultivated for about eight thousand years, first in Peru and in northern parts of Bolivia. It made its way to Europe via the Spanish conquistadors around 1570, and although the Spanish planted potatoes, they mainly used them as livestock feed because they multiply easily.

The role of the potato as an ingredient and food source fluctuates depending on the region and continues to evolve over time. In many parts of the word, it remains a vital crop. While Europe, particularly Eastern and Central Europe, remains one of the highest per capita producers in the world, recent years have seen the most rapid growth in Southern and Eastern Asia, where China and India have become the top producers globally.[13] The potato is considered the fourth most important crop behind corn, wheat, and rice.[14] It's versatile and adaptable to many different climates. After all, the potato was the first vegetable to be grown in space. The

2015 film *The Martian*, although fictional, highlighted scientific work to grow potatoes even in extreme environments.[15]

Beyond chips and french fries, potatoes are also an ingredient in alcoholic beverages like vodka, poteen, and aquavit.[16] The world produces almost four hundred million tons of potatoes every year. China, Europe, and India are the largest producers in the world. Canada remains a small player globally, producing roughly five million tons a year, but it is one of the few commodities that is grown in all provinces throughout the country. Canada has been a world leader in the production of seed potatoes for almost one hundred years and is the fifth largest seed potato exporter in the world. There are about 150 potato seed varieties registered in Canada.

Any dish that uses the potato is influenced by its internationalization, yet it is difficult to see how the popularity of poutine has increased the consumption of fries in general. For poutine, french fries are its main anchor, the foundation of all other ingredients. While there are multiple varieties of poutines, the french fries are a constant.

French fries originated in Europe in the seventeenth century, though whether they were invented in France or Belgium is not known. Looking at the facts, Belgium appears to have a stronger case. One origin story claims that the french fry began in Namur, Belgium, a French-speaking district. Namur is located by the River Meuse, where the people caught fish and fried them. One year, when the river froze over, the people began frying potatoes instead of fish, and the french fry was born.[17]

The Canadian champion for fries is arguably McCain Foods, based in Florenceville-Bristol, New Brunswick, the self-proclaimed "French fry capital of the world." Fries had started to become internationally popular after American and Canadian soldiers discovered them in Belgium after World War I, but McCain Foods truly made french fries famous and accessible in Canada, growing to become the "world's largest manufacturer of frozen French fries."[18] Today, McCain supplies more than 20 per cent of the fries consumed in China, but back in 1957, when McCain Foods first began selling frozen fries, it set the stage for Fernand Lachance to create the poutine with fries and cheese in Warwick, Quebec. Poutine may have originated in Quebec, but it's the entrepreneurial know-how of Atlantic Canada that has made a difference for the dish.

In England, fries (or "chips") are associated with fried fish. In Canada, fries are associated with poutine, but we have seen several varieties of fries over the years. Many are the standard shoestring or julienne cut, some still have the skin on them, McCain's fries are often "crinkle cut," and rustic wedges are popular, too. Some are even made from sweet potatoes, which are not really within the potato family. In fact, the sweet potato is part of the morning glory family. Some poutines use deep-fried fries. There are so many ways to cut and fry the potato for a poutine. Unlike cheese curds, not one method is preferred or dominant for poutine. Fries, however, remain its foundation.

Gravy and Innovation: A Fusion of Bliss

Sauces and gravies have been around since Ancient Greece. It was French cooking that took sauces to the next level and explored different flavours and options. Gravy is often made from the juices that run naturally from meat during cooking. These juices are then thickened with wheat flour or corn starch. For poutine, the type of sauce chosen was gravy, but before poutine became popular, it did not really have its own gravy. It borrowed its gravy from roasted or barbecued chicken, which was becoming popular in the 1950s. Many restaurants continue to use these gravy bases today.

The gravy, if done correctly, is what brings a poutine together. It mixes things up and enhances the flavours for the other ingredients. With poutine, the gravy melts the cheese curds so they can blend with the fries, creating a superb fusion of bliss. Poutine's history tells us that the sauce was the last ingredient added to poutine. It is also the only ingredient of the three that isn't enjoyed on its own. That fact is certainly not trivial.

However, there's little agreement about the gravy on poutine. Unlike cheese curds and fries, some people believe a poutine is fine without the sauce. Fernand Lachance, the father of poutine, believed a poutine should never have sauce. That would become a key moment in the evolution of the dish, from 1957 to 1964 (which I'll return to later). Lachance first served poutine without the gravy until his wife, Germaine Lachance, made her historic contribution by adding a ketchup-based sauce. It was "more of a barbeque sauce, whose ingredients included brown sugar, ketchup and Worcestershire sauce."[19] Historically, poutine is made with thick beef gravy. We see this when we take a closer look at Jean-Paul Roy's contribution to poutine.

Roy realized that a sauce would make all the difference, and as a trained saucier he was able to come up with the best formula for his poutine. His contribution changed everything. The poutine at Roy Jucep has a unique sweet flavour, which you have to taste in order to understand how a sauce can offer a different experience and transform poutine. To this day, his recipe remains a secret. Ashton Leblond, another early contributor to poutine, also insists that his recipe remain a secret. Of the three ingredients, the gravy is the one that is most intriguing. I've tasted all sorts of gravies during my travels – wine-based, beef-based, chicken-based, spaghetti sauce, tortilla sauce and salsa – you name it. Different gravies/sauces create different varieties of poutine.

Getting the right gravy for poutine is an art. Everyone has an opinion, and everyone has a different idea of what gravy and poutine should taste like. The stakes are high: gravy can spoil a poutine's taste and texture. The amount of gravy is as hotly debated as the kind. Some poutines are like soup with too much gravy, causing the fries to become soggy and unpleasant to eat. The right balance is always critical when preparing a poutine.

Poutine Varieties

My travels have made me realize that a lot of people know what poutine is. Restaurants, regions, and nations make versions of poutine that reflect their cultures. While the main ingredients of poutine are generally readily available around the world, they will not taste the same. Furthermore, additional ingredients create hundreds of variations around the world.

Yet the most common version is the traditional, with its three ingredients. It is still the top seller and the most recognized by lovers of poutine. Other versions include at least four ingredients. The most common additional ingredient found in poutine is the hot dog. It is often referred to as "hot dog poutine." Another common ingredient found in poutine is bacon. Bacon, onions, Swiss cheese, and sour cream as toppings make connections between poutine and steak. Another ingredient often seen on menus offering poutine is pepperoni, making the link with pizza, of course. "La Galvaude," with peas and chicken, is another version we have seen, which is heavily influenced by Ashton, the famous restaurant chain in Quebec. For some, this is not a poutine, but a perfect blend of creamy sauce, tender pieces of chicken, peas, and crispy fries. "Galvaude" means "disorder," "to mix things up," "to compromise something," even "to waste." Whichever definition you prefer, "Galvaude" is certainly an appropriate word to describe poutine.

Corn dogs are another ingredient you can find in poutine; I've also seen a combination of ground beef, bacon, onions, fried pickles, and Caesar salad dressing. One Mexican version includes ingredients such as bacon, red onions, guacamole, onion rings, and chipotle sauce. Another has beans and black olives. Some meat lovers opt for a combination between ground beef, pepperoni, and bacon. Spices, ground beef, smoked meat, spicy sausage, and merguez sausage are added to create a punchy version of poutine. Pork is also added to poutine. Pulled pork, creamy coleslaw, and sour cream is a popular combination. Apples are often added to the mixture to give it a sweeter taste. In Montreal, in particular, smoked meat is a popular ingredient, often added with other types of meats or with onions and plain mustard. And of course, vegans can get their own version with vegan cheese and vegan sauce. Above all, familiar ingredients can make poutine less intimidating and more accessible to the uninitiated.

As mentioned earlier, restaurants or chefs have given poutine different names over the years to try to entice customers to eat certain versions. Like most fast food, names are used to provoke or to describe the experience in a dramatic fashion. Menus from all over the world reveal some strange names. For example, the "Hangover" is a combination of "house fries, fresh curds, cheddar cheese, bacon, Italian sausage, seasoned ground beef, 911 sauce, a fried egg, and BBQ sauce."[20] This version is served by a restaurant called Poutineville, a franchise that has about ten restaurants in Montreal. The "Godfather" is another interesting name used for a poutine. It's no surprise that the "Godfather" poutine has an Italian bent to it. House fries, fresh curds, Italian sausage, roasted red peppers, green onions, meat sauce, and melted mozzarella. Greek-style "Zeus" poutine has ingredients such as fries, fresh cheese curds, feta cheese, gyro, tomatoes, red onions, green onions, and red wine sauce.[21] Some places will also offer a "sugar shack" special with ham and maple syrup. Not for everyone, of course.

Some classic dishes have also found a way to merge with poutine over the years. The "donair" special can also be found in many different locations. Invented in Halifax sometime in the 1970s, the donair has become quite popular over the years. Typically, a "donair-poutine" is a combination of traditional poutine mixed with donair meat, garlic sweet sauce, red onion, and tomatoes.[22] Thousands of different poutine versions now exist, and creativity has meant that some versions are more popular than others. To date I have been unable to find a Halal poutine, but that doesn't mean it's not being served somewhere.

An interesting side note is that there are some poutines that are being given political names or at least look at the dish through a political lens. For instance, one poutine is called the "Nuclear Threat." This refers to North Korea's dictator, Kim Jong-Un, and uses Korean beef. Another noteworthy fact is that some restaurants serve dessert poutine, which consists of fries – sometimes fried bread sticks – served with caramel, ice cream, or chocolate.

One subtle difference between poutine served in Quebec versus other places is the size options. In most places around the world, poutine is available in only one size. In Quebec, poutine is often offered in several sizes – small, regular, or large – so it can be shared. A large poutine becomes a convenient size for two, three, or even four. In many places, a poutine is served in a regular-sized portion, which makes sharing a little more difficult. Poutineville offers a fifteen-pound heart-attack size. This option is to be shared, of course. In 2019, Warwick, Quebec, beat the world record for making the largest poutine in history, weighing 3,034 kilograms. It was large enough that over six thousand people could share it![23]

Poutine remains paradoxical: it has three essential ingredients, which are easy to get wrong, while at the same time, it has been exported around the world, developing vastly different versions in each new location to suit local tastes. The following chapters will examine how this came to be, as well as poutine's future.

CHAPTER FOUR

Why the First Time You Eat Poutine Matters

Taste is a construct. Everyone has different taste buds formed by their unique experiences and cultures, where they come from, their habits, their preferences, even their values. Taste is both arbitrary and quite personal. When you eat poutine for the first time influences how you see and taste the dish in the future. When you order it again, you expect it to taste a certain way, the way it *should* taste. This expectation is impossible to meet for several reasons.

Most don't remember the first time they ate poutine. I certainly don't, at least not clearly. What I do know is that I was with my family, and that first experience shaped my expectations for the years to come. International students experience poutine as part of their initiation to Canadian culture. That initial introduction will frame their opinion about poutine. Several tourism websites encourage people to try poutine when visiting Canada, especially in Quebec.

Many will recommend that poutine needs to be eaten in order to really experience the Canadian lifestyle.

In many parts of the world, poutine is served with different ingredients and has become something completely different from what Quebecers know in "La Belle Province." As a dish becomes internationalized, this is often the case. Hawaiian pizza, for instance, was invented in Canada. For most Italians, putting ham and pineapple on a pizza is unheard of, yet it happens nevertheless. For poutine, fries tend to be more or less consistent around the world, but there is a shocking amount of variation in the cheeses and sauces used. Sampling poutine in Cleveland, Ohio, I was surprised to find it served with parmesan powder. After talking to individuals in the city, I came to understand that this was quite normal to them. Why is that, I wondered?

To understand this, we need to look at some research in psychology. A meal is "the natural psychological/ecological unit of eating."[1] In other words, most of us will consider a meal as the unit of analysis. We either like a meal or we do not, and rarely, if ever, do we dissect the meal into parts.[2] Our routine meals are experienced too many times over the years, which makes it difficult to recall the actual experience of any of them specifically.[3] As for eating something for the first time, we may remember it, but that memory becomes cloudy over time. Each time we eat that meal again, the brain has a chance to recalibrate its memories. Ultimately, when we decide to purchase groceries or order something at a restaurant, we can only draw from our subjective memories of the original eating experiences.[4] This is key when remembering how poutine tastes or what it should taste like.

In the short term, we remember details about our experience. We recall how the gravy or cheese tasted; in other words, we break the meal into parts. However, many years later, we are only able to recall whether we enjoyed the meal or not. This memory will make us either a poutine lover or a poutine hater. Most importantly, though, that first experience will define how a meal should be experienced and will mark your long-term memory.

Some interesting research in psychology suggests that initial bites matter. Whether the experience is pleasant or not, the first few bites are critical in the experience of a meal. That's why most servers will come and visit your table and ask if everything is satisfactory. It's all about the psychology of taste.[5]

There is, however, hope in changing our memories about the food we eat over time. This is what some call working memory. Our working memory can be improved via adaptive training. For example, if you eat a poutine for the first time, say in Tokyo, it will be served in a certain way. This poutine will dictate how you believe a poutine should taste. But if you relocate to a market where poutine is served differently, your taste and memory for the dish may change.[6] You can basically train yourself into liking or disliking a particular dish, but the process needs to be deliberate and to extend over several months, perhaps years.

Another aspect of this kind of memory is the way a meal is eaten.[7] If someone eats a meal slowly, that person is more likely to remember the experience more vividly.

When eating a poutine for the first time, the social aspect of the experience can be overwhelming.[8] If you are in a large group of people, your choice of food can be influenced as you may feel compelled to order one; alternately, for ease and expediency, you may decide to share one with other people.[9] You may eat your first poutine quickly, or not, depending on the context and where you are when eating it for the first time. If you eat it very quickly, you may be giving yourself a chance to redefine what poutine means to you in the future.

We rationalize everything, even food. "Making sense of food is a relational process between consumer and food, and it brings together a host of knowledges and experiences, that inform food preferences and the choices made when buying food."[10] Our pre-set knowledge influences how we consume food and how we taste it as well.[11] These experiences can be categorized into three different taste experiences that contribute to the palatability of foods: sweet, salty, and umami (savouriness, literally "deliciousness" in Japanese). In other words, the perception of these basic tastes in foods tends to promote their intake. In the case of poutine, saltiness is the main driver in terms of flavour, but some variance may occur when ingredients are added or changed.[12] This has a profound impact on how people consume food on a regular basis and also affects their preferences.

Technically speaking, tastes, expectations, and food preferences have a lot to do with dopamine. "The association of taste with wanting food ... is related to the release of dopamine in the meso-limbic circuitry of the brain. Dopamine release due to [food taste] is phasic and contingent on stimulus novelty."[13] This mental reflex to food develops over time. "Dopamine release also has a role in associative learning with food."[14] That process allows us to remember tastes and link them to specific experiences and dishes. Therefore, when someone experiences poutine for the first time, that taste defines what poutine should and ought to taste like for that person.

There is a social aspect to taste as well. This is apparent in the interactions between consumers and the person serving the dish. Furthermore, poutine's prominence affects our experience of it, whether it is just a side dish among others or the main dish on the menu of an establishment. Some studies have argued that the way a dish is served and presented impacts the way it tastes.[15] One particularly intriguing study points to how taste expectations are mediated by the influence of the colour, shape, and size of the plate on which it is served; that is, actual perceived taste was influenced by participants' expectations concerning colour and flavour associations.[16] Participants expected that the taste for the same food product would be more intense or different when it was served in a different plate or bowl; they also actually experienced the same food product as different. In other words, it seems reasonable to posit that visual cues influence both taste expectations and how the food actually tastes.[17]

Where we eat the dish also influences how we see the dish. Most people won't eat poutine at home, on their own. Poutine is often consumed outside the home in a social setting. The concept of place has been frequently used to explore how people relate to and find meaning in their environment, particularly in the field of human geography.[18] Place should be considered as a fluid entity, to a certain extent, as opposed to something that is, for example, defined by organizational processes such as a restaurant or a home. "Place links people to things in the world and allows us to explore how we inhabit and experience the world we live in."[19] Eating a dish outside the home has much to do with the environment, in addition to the actual taste of the product.[20]

Our nose can play tricks on us as well. Scent is a very strong influencer of food choice and taste, and many people know, through sense memory, how a poutine smells. A traditional poutine tastes like fries and gravy. Cheese has a neutral scent and is rarely a factor. In certain cases, the gravy itself can be a dominating factor when it comes to smell. For example, a wine-based gravy, unlike a beef- or pork-based gravy, could dominate the olfactory experience and influence taste expectations. The food industry has used smell to entice us to eat certain foods, especially foods that may not be good for us.[21] It has generally been assumed that a food's aroma, when we inhale it before eating, determines how we will think about its flavour. Other research, however, "has shown that when we eat something, the odours that go up to our olfactory bulb from the back of the mouth are processed in a different part of the brain to the odours taken in when we put our nose near something and sniff."[22] That smell is stored somewhere in our brain and impacts how we experience the same product or dish the next time we eat it. Therefore, our first experience eating a poutine causes us to be quite critical of how other poutines are experienced in the future.

The First Time

Many people have a story about poutine, whether it is the first time they heard the word or the first time they partook. Many don't remember the first time they ate poutine, but they may have a memory of its taste. My first encounter with poutine was likely at L'Ami du Passant in my hometown of Farnham. But like many, I just don't remember exactly.

Typically, I would order something traditional, like a hot dog or hamburger. But all my friends were ordering a poutine, and so I did. I would not say that I loved my first experience, but it did leave an impression. It was like tasting pizza for the first time. Most won't remember when they ate pizza for the first time, but they generally want to eat it again. I felt the same about poutine. I didn't know poutine was invented in my home province, literally sixty minutes away from my hometown. And frankly, it would

Photo 4.1. L'Ami du Passant in Farnham, Quebec, my hometown, the location where I had my first poutine.

not have meant much if I had known at the time. Let's face it, fries, cheese curds, and gravy, big deal. Why make this a special event, really?

In those days, poutine was not known outside our world, but we didn't know any better. It's when I joined the military and travelled across Canada that I realized poutine was unknown. Not one place offered poutine in the cities I visited, except for the obscure fast-food shack right outside the military base. I remember seeing a sign that said "Poutine Here" in Shearwater, BC, about 150 metres from the base's entrance. The message was clearly intended for homesick French officers visiting the base for a while. That's when I realized that the rest of the world had no idea what poutine was.

I wanted to collect some stories from people about their first encounter with poutine, so I reached out to the public. I received over a hundred notes through social media and spoke to roughly twenty-five people. I randomly asked if they remembered when they had eaten poutine for the first time. Some stories were quite entertaining. Some of the stories were telling. The military system appears to have played a huge role in making poutine known around the country. Whether you were in the service or a base brat (someone who is raised on a base), poutine played a part. Here's one reaction I received: "I ate my first poutine in the late '70s as a kid growing up at CFB [Canadian Forces Base] Valcartier. There was a takeout called Le Cartier. The poutine was served in those deep hot tinfoil dishes with a paper lid. They were rink fries avec cheese curds and gravy. So good!"

CFB Valcartier is in Quebec City, where poutine has been sold for years. As a former officer, I can certainly relate.

Another person had an experience at one of Canada's military bases outside the country. They remembered that "it was 1990 at CFB Lahr in Germany. A friend who had lived in Quebec for many years saw it on the menu and told me I had to try it. I hadn't even heard of it being from an English part of Canada. I'm glad it's offered everywhere now." It makes sense. Most military folks are away from home, so the Department of National Defence has always tried to offer food that their personnel can relate to, to make them feel at home. Poutine was served in many ways, the tinfoil bowl with a paper lid being the most common way.

Someone else also commented on the packaging, but this time, hockey was involved: "I won a 'grosse poutine' at Ashton in Quebec City at the end of a hockey season (can you tell I'm Québécois?). Lasagna-size tin container with cardboard cover, one-fifth of it got eaten by my eighty-pound self." Sports, specifically hockey, were the cause of many people discovering poutine for the first time. Most arenas have a place where you can buy fries and other junk food. These canteens and restaurants, like Ashton, would sponsor events and give free poutine to kids and adults alike for them to discover the dish.

Many stories were about when people had visited Quebec for the first time or moved to the province. Some said that they had their first "real poutine" when they were visiting Quebec: "My first time eating REAL poutine was only a few years ago just near Château Frontenac. Cubed potatoes and real cheese curds. It was amazing." People from outside Canada also had interesting things to say about poutine. Some Americans added their experiences to the discussion.

They often related to what they knew and compared poutine with a dish from back home to explain how different it was: "Omg yes. Raised in Arkansas chili cheese fries were a way of life. Being introduced to their more refined Canadian first cousin was a mash up of a childhood favorite in a more sociably acceptable plating." And: "I don't remember my first steps and I don't remember my first poutine … but they probably didn't happen too far apart."

Many said that once you tasted poutine, it was difficult to see fries the same way again. The combination is that memorable. For many Canadians, Canada is not their country of origin. Many immigrated to Canada and discovered poutine for the first time. One wanted to share her experience with poutine at a young age: "One month after immigrating to Canada! Sixteen-year-old me was blown away by the poutine (described as fries with cheese and gravy) offered at my high school cafeteria in Richmond Hill, ON. Still one of my favourite teenage memories." This person's experience is interesting, especially for today. I'm not sure if poutine is served in a school cafeteria anymore, given how unhealthy it is. But people remembered, and it made a difference in their lives. According to Allan Woods, "we now celebrate poutine, create food festivals around it and dress it up in lobster, pulled pork, foie gras, curry sauce, merguez,"[23] you name it. However, for much of its history, poutine has been sneered at as cheap and unhealthy. Woods explains that "poutine was embraced neither by Quebec's elite, who looked to France for their culinary references, nor English Canada," which ridiculed the meal as a one-way ticket to the grave.[24]

Poutine has since travelled across military bases, hockey rinks, to the United States, and around the world, getting more and more popular. Along that journey, poutine evolved from a rural Quebec dish to a staple of Canadian cuisine. Not to everyone's liking, sure, but poutine has reached stardom.

PART II

The Bedrock

CHAPTER FIVE

With Poutine, History Matters

I never really appreciated poutine's history until I left home. When I was growing up, my mom cooked and made sure every holiday was special. For her, the best way to make anything feel and look special was with her cooking. Some food was quite good, and we looked forward to eating some dishes again. Her macaroni salad and rolled sandwiches with cherries in the middle were unforgettable, while her turkey and meat pie, on the other hand, were mediocre. Her dishes always played a part in these traditions. While they weren't perfect, they framed memories, created tastes, and even informed certain values. That's how traditions were and are made at home.

Food traditions are an important part of our histories, and they can say a great deal about a culture, about how the past has affected us as a society. Food and agriculture directly or indirectly affect "labour, immigration, gender, race and ethnicity, community, public health, transnational history, colonial history, and urban history" – wherever you look, food leaves its mark.[1] Indeed, food culture is a lens through which we can understand a culture, whether we study restaurants as "the nexus between production, consumption, distribution, procurement, and representation"[2] or step back to examine broader trends.

For many, food is a gateway to a career, a lifestyle, and most importantly, hope. In fact, one person in five had their first job working in the agri-food sector.[3] I worked on farms during my youth, so I'm one of them. My wife's first job was at Rôtisserie St-Hubert. Many immigrants find work in the food service industry, and through food they make a living and come to feel accepted in their new home. In Canada, the role of immigrant cultures affecting our food cannot be overemphasized. Almost 21 per cent of Canadians are immigrants, one of the highest percentages in the world.[4] Every year, hundreds of thousands of immigrants come to Canada, and the country relies on them to compensate for its demographic shortfalls and gaps in the labour force.[5] Immigrants open ethnic restaurants and specialty stores, thereby introducing Canadians to many foreign foods, such as perogies, sushi, pho, and falafel, among others.

As a growing number of Canadians develop palates for new cuisines, food has become a way for people to journey beyond borders and share more complex, inclusive, and truthful stories about Canada and its culinary past. Canadians are travelling more, expanding our view of food. Our tastes are more globalized than ever before.

Many Canadians don't know what a Canadian dish looks like, or what Canada's contribution to the culinary arts has been. They may know a few dishes, but there is little pride attached to them. Canadians tend to enjoy food that came from abroad.

Our Canadian food culture is young and fragmented, which makes it hard for many of us to describe what Canadian cuisine is. The rise in popularity of some foods has partially filled this gap, such as the BeaverTail pastry or maple syrup, which has always been around but has been popularized recently with better marketing at airports, restaurants, and shops. Poutine, similar to maple syrup, now stands out as a dish closely associated with Canadian cuisine. Canadians travelling abroad would notice this association as poutine can be found in many places across the globe. There are, of course, many interesting food cultures that belong to the Indigenous Peoples in Canada, but due to ongoing and systemic intolerance, most Canadians have a very poor understanding of what they are, other than bannock (a kind of fried bread) or smoked salmon. There's still much reconciliation required for Canadians to understand and celebrate these cultures and their food.

Several years ago, when I was travelling in Europe, Asia, South America, and other places, poutine was not part of the conversation when discussing Canadian cuisine. And frankly, I barely spoke about Canadian cuisine. Whenever I'm in another country, the last thing I want to do is talk about what we eat at home. I don't think that the people I met wanted to hear much about what we ate in Canada, either. I've always wanted to discover new tastes, new dishes, and how people value food in general.

This lack of pride or interest in Canadian cuisine that I and many others felt may have deeper roots. Canadians may feel that poutine is not worthy of being called a Canadian creation, much less a culinary icon, due to its simplicity and unhealthy aspects.[6] One could almost argue that Canadians discriminate against poutine, unwilling to admit that our cuisine is represented by a sloppy junk food.

While writing this book, I had to go back and understand our history as a young country. As I understand it, Canada's historical evolution clearly influenced poutine's history. Much like poutine's path to glory, however, Canada's history has not always been pretty.

Canada's Dark History

Although most Canadians would agree that a perfect society does not exist, our Charter of Rights and Freedoms nevertheless sets out our core values of equality, freedom, democracy, multiculturalism, and Indigenous rights.[7] Our country does have a dark side, though, and a history of denial.[8] Indigenous Peoples, women, people of colour, 2SLGBTQI+ people, and other groups have experienced discrimination, marginalization, and oppression. Canadian history, as taught in schools, often refuses to admit the existence of systemic or structured inequalities. This is what Canada was and is today, to a certain extent, whether we like it or not. Government policies and practices in Canada have been prejudiced against Indigenous Peoples, immigrant communities, and many other minority groups.[9]

We can see Canada's dark history in the history of poutine. The dish came from a place where immigration was almost non-existent and xenophobia was widespread. In 1957, rural Quebec was white, male-dominated, and predominately Catholic, and people followed a similar mindset, shared the same values, and had their place in society. You were considered a good Catholic if you got married, had lots of kids, and went to church every Sunday. In rural communities, this is the norm, or at least it used to be.[10] To a certain extent, things are not much different today. Poutine came from a place where racism and intolerance abound. Until you leave the region, it's hard to realize how much diversity in thought and culture there can be. I wish it were different, but that's how things were. Of course, things have improved, but much work remains.

For many decades, Quebecers were having children, lots of children, especially in rural Quebec under the Catholic Church's doctrine. Immigration was not an issue, so until very recently Quebec was not faced with the need to accept differences. When it came to Indigenous communities, Quebec pretended they did not exist as they fell under the jurisdiction of the federal government. For many years, everyone was the same. While other parts of Canada dealt with complex issues of immigration, the rural communities in Quebec resisted change.

Early on in the history of colonial North America, ethnic and racial differences divided Indigenous peoples and settlers. The public as well as the government's attitude towards newcomers depended greatly on their national origin. Western Europeans were largely preferred, "followed by other White Christians, Jews, and at the bottom, non-Europeans peoples."[11] This same grading approach was used in both Canada and the United States. In the late nineteenth century, Canada, along with the United States, instituted a head tax on Chinese immigrants.[12] Countless measures were taken against specific groups trying to immigrate to Canada with the hope of living a better life. Canada, to a certain extent, has learned from its mistakes and adopted policies that are much less discriminatory. But there is a lot of work to be done. "Perhaps surprisingly, given the educational advantage of immigrants in Canada … immigrants in the United States fare better in the job market" than in Canada.[13]

Immigrants and Indigenous Peoples outside Quebec have learned to live with each other. However, there remain points of tension that remind us how complicated living together can be. With the exception of Montreal, Quebec never had to confront the effects of immigration until after the Quiet Revolution beginning in 1960, making it unique in Canada.[14] Quebec was comfortable until it had to deal with the reality of depopulation and rural abandonment, and only recently has the province dealt with immigration and its resultant cultural clashes. So in 1957, when Jean-Guy Lainesse made his famous request to mix cheese and fries, Quebec was still comfortable, still stagnant and homogeneous. Whether or not such a context led to poutine's creation is up for debate. It is, however, an interesting hypothesis.

Quebec's Political Context

In Quebec, politics is an obsession, to the point that families, like mine, have been divided by their political views. Unlike other Canadians, Quebecers are not afraid to talk about politics, at any time and anywhere. The separatist movement is complicated, but simply put, it is essentially about preserving a culture.[15] For most separatists, the state is the best mechanism through which to protect the interests of a nation. This mindset has influenced the history of the province for many, many years, including my youth and young adulthood.

It's almost impossible to talk about food without going into politics. Food and agriculture are inherently political, and context is always key when discussing food. Throughout history, political context has been an influential force in food, and it is still true today.[16] Food is "deeply meaningful for identity construction and the negotiation of social relations ... in imagined national food communities" and in the family ties around the dinner table.[17] Food, like politics, unites us, but in different ways.

Poutine was created when Maurice Duplessis was premier of Quebec (1936–9, 1944–59). Duplessis played a critical role in the social and economic evolution of the province, and while many outside Quebec will know who Duplessis was, few can appreciate how influential his tenure was in Quebec's history.

He died while in office in 1959 at the age of sixty-nine (1890–1959), after leading the province for almost twenty years. To this day, no one has served longer as premier of

Quebec than Maurice Duplessis. I was not alive to see how the province looked under his regime, but most of the literature on Quebec history and its politics is not kind to the man from Trois-Rivières. His era as leader of the province is seen as a period of great darkness (La Grande Noirceur). This term is still used today to signify how few could communicate or raise concerns about how the province was being governed. Most felt repressed, especially women, ethnic minorities, or anyone who was not a white Catholic man. Duplessis gave the Catholic Church a great deal of political attention and focused on rural economic development. However, he was very much against social progress, the rights of women, and Quebec nationalism. For the rest of Canada, he is likely seen as the most conservative premier the province has ever had.[18]

Essentially, "Quebec's Quiet Revolution of the 1960s was preceded by a decade of critical institutional and intellectual changes (Behiels). Urbanization and modernization of the provincial economy marked the 1950s prelude, processes which were guided by a nationalist reawakening."[19] That awakening became more real over the following two decades. The height of Quebec's socio-political and economic influence was likely between 1967 and 1980, when Montreal hosted Expo '67 and the Summer Olympic Games. I couldn't find any evidence that poutine played any part at either of the events, but it was a different time then. It was a time when most people in Quebec believed everything was possible, even the creation of a nation, the Quebec Republic. Over time though, the separatist movement became such a distraction that it consumed most of what Quebec had set out to achieve.

Ideologically, Quebec in the middle of the twentieth century focused on the elites and the intellectuals, those small pockets where power was concentrated. Societal changes were accompanied by a reappraisal of traditional social classes and how Quebec saw itself. An emerging francophone middle class that believed a new ideology was needed in a modern society challenged the old guard of Quebec's society. Intellectual thinkers and social critics; health, psychological, and educational experts; trade union activists and women's associations; and outspoken university students controlled the province's economic and social development agenda. Put simply, conservative ideals and priorities had precedent over liberal, progressive ones in those days.

The abrupt end to Duplessis's reign allowed the Quiet Revolution to occur and ushered in the welfare state that the province experienced for more than four decades. After Duplessis's death, the province went through a period of great uncertainty. Duplessis had a larger-than-life persona and controlled everything in government and society. His departure left a huge void. Quebec had two very short-term premiers in Paul Sauvé (1959–60, who also died in office of a heart attack after serving for only 112 days as premier) and Antonio Barrette (1960), before settling for Jean Lesage (1960–6). Lesage oversaw an era that was very different from the Duplessis years. In Quebec, the Quiet Revolution worked in sync with social movements in the United States. Socially, Quebec was changing fast.[20]

This was an interesting and tumultuous period in Quebec, but where does poutine fit in all this? Could the social suppression experienced under Duplessis have somehow led to the creation of poutine in rural Quebec? The need to indulge, creating an escape by way of a dish that has nothing to do with compliance? Poutine breaks all the social and physical rules we can think of imposing on ourselves. Poutine could represent the political left and a rebellious way of looking at our society, or it could be a statement coming from a group that felt disenfranchised for many years. It could also be seen as a product of social isolation, the closeness and relative insularity of the communities from which it emerged. It's just a hypothesis, but food is certainly a way to allow a group to express themselves.

At the same time, years of political suppression have made many Quebecers feel that it's inappropriate to brag. In some circumstances, it's almost openly discouraged and frowned upon.[21] Quebecers are known not to show off wealth, and success cannot be expressed in any tangible ways. Unlike other parts of the country, looking like someone with more means than the average person is gauche, as most would think that the person is either a criminal or someone who does not give back enough to support the community. That is the Catholic Church's legacy, and Duplessis embraced that philosophy to a tee. Many successful businesspeople in Quebec still feel this way.

This modest mindset continues to have an impact on Quebec society today. When travelling around the province, I could see that few people really appreciated what was happening to Quebec's most famous dish. It's now internationally known, one of Quebec's greatest exports, and people from all over the world serve the dish, even if they've added their own special twist to it. Quebec remains inward-looking and not necessarily aware of what is happening globally, even if it concerns its own culture, paying more attention to France than English Canada or the United States.[22]

As I noted earlier, I have lived in many parts of the country, and there is no doubt that most Canadians love Quebec and its culture. They have embraced poutine like it was their own. No judgment, just joy, indulgence, and pleasure. Joie de vivre! Politics aside, Canadians enjoy being with Quebecers and poutine reminds them of Quebec and its culture. For most Canadians, it's an important feature of their shared cultural experience. Perhaps due to this, English Canada appears to be aware of and even embracing poutine's global success more than Quebec is. While one society has been so inward-looking, the other is embracing what is considered one of Canada's best culinary creations.

I have been fortunate to have lived in most provinces in the country. In fact, by the time I was twenty-one, I had visited all ten provinces and one territory. In an era where vacations to Cancun or weekend visits to New York were more in vogue, visiting the entire country was not common. My travels across Canada have provided me with an idea of what this country is all about, especially the food culture of the rest of Canada. As a young man from Quebec, I was amazed by the beauty of the country and how different it was from where I grew up, but I was particularly struck by how different food was and how quickly it seemed to be changing.

During my childhood, the Quebec food culture was carefully preserved. It meant something to a great deal of people.

In the late 1980s, though, the traditional restaurants serving tourtière (meat pie), soupe aux pois (pea soup), ragoût de boulettes (meatball stew), and cretons (cracklings from pork fat) were almost all gone. Most of these restaurants were visited by foreigners and tourists. The sharp decline in restaurants serving traditional dishes was offset by the proliferation of American fast-food, ethnic, and gourmet restaurants. This was surprising to see given how protective Quebec and Quebecers are about the agricultural roots of the province.

In rural Quebec, there was no better way to celebrate Quebec's cuisine than at country fairs. They played a big role in how people celebrated nature's bounty and food. It was the same in many parts of the country, and Quebec was no exception. I remember visiting fairs when I was a child with my parents and brothers, the unheralded Brome Fair in the Eastern Townships, most of all. The St-Hyacinthe country fair was the largest in the province, and it is still running today. But it has changed over the years from a country-folk fair to an urban gathering of food styles and rides. It is not at all what it was. Of course, as a child, the only thing we wanted to do was go on the rides, and we did not give much thought to the food or the crafts that were displayed. Also close to my home was Bedford, the home of the oldest country fair in Canada. It has been around for almost two hundred years. Fairs are meant to bring people together, after days and weeks of hard labour at the end of the summer, when things start to calm down just before harvest.

It was quite typical to see local products celebrated at village festivals throughout Quebec as icons of local identity.

Poutine was there, but it was not overly obvious. For these events, it was critical to reflect Quebec's identity and spirit. In those days, separatism was quite vibrant. So, the need to nurture pride and self-preservation was very much part of everyday life. For as long as I can remember, my family was always federalist (that is what we called ourselves), but it didn't matter. In those days, you were either a separatist or a federalist. That's how it worked. It was widely accepted that the cities were mostly federalist, and the rural regions were separatist. Because I was French, young, and living in the country, most assumed that I was a separatist, but I never was, and I never will be. Today, separatism is mostly seen as a project for a generation that has grown older. Younger folks are more globally aware and are accepting the fact that creating a separate nation within Canada is not the best solution. What's interesting is how poutine became this emblematic symbol around the world, creating its own "nation" while, at home, there was so much infighting about the creation of another "nation."

I do remember one moment in time, May 20, 1980, the day of the first Quebec referendum.[23] I was ten years old and had no idea what a referendum was. I remember my father telling me that he voted "no" for us and for our generation as we watched René Lévesque give his concession speech. It is a moment I will never forget. I could tell the separatist movement divided the province and many families. Even in school, you were almost encouraged not to talk to kids who were part of "separatist" families. I could tell the referendum was a difficult thing for my father, who felt torn between wanting to preserve his culture, our culture, and safeguarding our country. What remained constant was that my parents had resolved to teach us where we came from. The one way to do it was to visit fairs and the countryside. It was fine by me if I could go on rides and eat some candy. And, of course, later I encountered poutine.

In recent years, country fairs have all but disappeared in Quebec. Village festivals no longer stir up the same enthusiasm as they did in the past. It was almost as if Quebec culture was fading away along with its food. Compared to Europe and Asia's great number of restaurants dedicated to local cuisine, what is most striking in Quebec culture is the number of ethnic restaurant customers. Montreal, Quebec City, and many other cities and towns in the province have restaurants that serve food we would not have even known about twenty years ago. Traditions and heritage have taken a back seat to more international, cosmopolitan tastes, and what is foreign is viewed as hip, in fashion, desirable, and often associated with modernity. It is cool to go to places where menus are novel and unique. Small and strange is good; familiar and predictable, less so. It is not a stretch to say that food culture in Quebec today is largely defined by cuisine from other parts of the world.

Fairs were the primary way for farmers and country folks to get together, relax, have fun, and eat. But junk food has also played an important role at these fairs. Hungry families headed for food concessions and junk food. Fairs are known, particularly in America, for serving unhealthy, greasy dishes, and part of the fun seems to be serving as many calories as possible. Fairgoers don't seem to mind; they even look forward to it. Most fairgoers ate the same thing every year, for nostalgic reasons. Our family did the same. We ate this bizarre-looking hamburger with a weird mixture of cooked onions and peppers put on top of the patty. We only ordered it when we were at the fair. No poutine, just a disgusting-looking hamburger with regular fries. We ate these calorific meals on small tables outside. It was a family meal, free from concerns about dignity and class, and we loved it. Flies flew everywhere, and every surface was dirty, which seems rather strange today with our concern for food safety and hygiene. My parents never thought twice about cleanliness, except for our clothes and faces when we were in public. I relish these memories and have tried to take the same approach with my own children … within reason.

My wife, children, and I have visited fairs in many parts of the country: Ontario, the Prairies, and the Atlantic Provinces. They are always fun but never quite the same as they were in Quebec. Country fairs outside of Quebec feel like fundraisers, an excuse to get people together on a given weekend. There's food, but nothing out of the ordinary. Food trucks, hot dog stands, and that's about it. In Quebec, fairs served a distinct and important purpose. Despite how important fairs were to Quebec's discovery of itself, poutine never played a central role in these events, which is odd given the dish's rural origins. I can't think of a better way to celebrate this dish than during these events.

Even when poutine became popular, it was viewed as something of a joke, something you added to the menu at a fast-food joint, but little more. Poutine had its place in the food industry, that's it. Over time though, the world has embraced poutine, creating a kind of "Poutine Nation."

"Poutine Nation" is more than a plate of fries, cheese curds, and gravy – it's a borderless cultural idea rooted in resilience, adaptability, and belonging. It represents a shared identity forged not by geography or politics, but by a humble dish that has transcended its origins.

Born in rural Quebec, poutine was once ridiculed as unsophisticated and low-class. Yet it endured. Over decades, it evolved from a local curiosity into a symbol of cultural pride. As it spread across Canada and eventually around the world, poutine morphed into something far greater: a unifying experience that defied language, class, and borders.

Poutine Nation, then, is not a place. It's a mindset. It's about embracing the ordinary and making it extraordinary. It reflects how something once dismissed as déclassé can become a culinary ambassador – uniting food trucks in Montreal, diners in Saskatoon, gastropubs in London, and late-night street vendors in Tokyo.

In a fragmented world, Poutine Nation invites us to find common ground in comfort food. It stands for cultural humility, transformation through adversity, and a celebration of the unpretentious. It's about pride without pretension—and the idea that something as simple as melted curds and gravy can tell a story of identity, inclusion, and quiet resistance.

In fact, poutine's success and international notoriety are very much due to people not living in Quebec. In other words, poutine became famous despite how Quebecers discriminated against it, for a while, despite its birth in a stuffy, stagnant age.

CHAPTER SIX

Cooking, Religions, and History

Many have wondered why dishes and recipes exist in the first place.[1] As a species, we started recording and exchanging recipes thousands of years ago, roughly twenty-two thousand years in fact. Cooking kills harmful bacteria and makes food easier to digest, especially grains, which were the main staples in ancient civilizations.[2] Very early on, social rank and religion played a role in cooking and meals.[3]

The extravagant cuisine of the elites in Greece, Persia, and Rome emphasized the widening disparity between their luxurious meals and the humble fare of commoners.[4] As elites were eating meat, lower classes had to settle for grains and raw fruits and vegetables. Animal protein remained a luxury in many parts of the world.

Faith and organized religion have been strong influences on cuisines around the world and throughout history, giving symbolic meaning to bread, pork, seafood, wine, etc. Religion, as we know, plays a role in our identity and structure within our cultural systems. Religion has also provided rules around eating cooked and raw foods in certain cultures. For instance, Hebrew dietary restrictions control one's identity in the context of keeping the Hebrew tribes clean. One dietary restriction is the prohibition on the consumption of pork. The ways foods are eaten, or not eaten, are dictated by taboos and sacred myths. Cooking for the gods was the initial intent of the sacrificial feasts that were common in many cultures three thousand years ago,[5] but food can also be viewed as a force for good and unity.

Judaism has strict dietary laws that are intertwined with identity and lifestyle. The Hindu caste system determines who can cook for whom and who can eat with whom. The altar in Christian churches lays out the sacred meal of Christ's body. Muslims fast during Ramadan as one of the five pillars of Islam. In each case, food is interconnected with one's relationship to holiness.

I had the pleasure of visiting Israel a few years ago. The experience reinforced my understanding of food's relationship with the sacred. I was there on a business trip but had a few days to discover the country. Tel Aviv looked like any other beautiful European city, and religion was everywhere. I arrived at my hotel on a Saturday, which is the Sabbat. Nobody works in Israel on Saturdays. To check in, I had to see a clerk in some obscure back room to give him my credit card and go through normal formalities. I was hungry, so I asked if I could go to the hotel restaurant to get a quick bite to eat. Oddly, the clerk did not respond. I understood why later.

As I entered the hotel restaurant, I saw an incredible buffet. I walked around and was so impressed by the different kinds of dishes I saw laid out. There were many dishes I had never seen before, and I had no idea what they were. As I began to fill my plate, an employee from the hotel came by to see me and asked if I was comfortable paying the $300 fee to eat from the buffet. Not wanting to pay the exorbitant price, I discreetly left. As I was exiting the restaurant, I realized I was the only one who was not part of a large group, a family. It was then that I remembered that it was Sabbat, and I clearly was not Jewish. I was a travelling stranger in the holy city.

As I continued on to Jerusalem, I learned and appreciated how protective the Jewish people are of their traditions and habits, especially relating to food. As I left my hotel in search of food, I was impressed by the beauty of Jerusalem. After wandering for a bit, I stopped at a little restaurant to eat something. As I normally do when I travel, I didn't look at the menu and, instead, asked the server to pick and choose a dish for me. They brought me a local dish, a salad. It was a salat katzutz, an Israeli salad with chopped cucumber, diced tomato, onion, cucumber, and bell or chili peppers. I was told that it has been described as the most well-known Israeli dish, sort of Israel's poutine.

The next morning, I took a tour from a man named Harry, who was originally from Montreal. The first place we visited was the site on which the Last Supper was said to have taken place almost two thousand years ago, although nobody knows for certain where the exact location is. It was an open but very simple room, all in marble. The room has a small niche for Muslim prayer called a *mihrab*, which dates back to the sixteenth century.[6] Besides being the setting of the Last Supper, "this 'upper room' is also believed to be the site of the descent of the Spirit on Pentecost. Interestingly, the room is located directly above the traditional (but very probably unhistorical) tomb of King David."[7]

Food has always played a central role in Christianity, and Harry, my guide, wanted to make sure I understood that. Some Christian churches teach that bread represents the body of Christ, and wine represents the blood of Christ. The story "Jesus Feeds the Five Thousand" is also known as the "miracle of the five loaves and two fish." The Gospels tell of Jesus performing a great miracle of multiplying two fish and five loaves of bread to feed a crowd of five thousand in Tabgha. It is difficult to underestimate how powerful a symbol food has been, and continues to be, for religions around the world.

Indeed, Christianity transformed the cuisines of Europe and the Americas[8] by reshaping when, what, and how people ate through its liturgical calendar, moral teachings, and global expansion. Fasting periods like Lent encouraged the development of fish-based and vegetarian dishes, while feast days such as Christmas and Easter gave rise to rich culinary traditions centred on specific foods like lamb, puddings, or sweet breads. Monasteries played a crucial role in preserving and advancing food practices, including winemaking, cheesemaking, and agriculture. As Christianity spread through colonization, it introduced Old World staples like wheat, grapes, cattle, horses, and pigs to the Americas – often tied to religious rituals – while also influencing or suppressing Indigenous food customs. Overall, Christianity wove spiritual meaning into food, shaping Western culinary traditions for centuries.

Its influence was strong until the seventeenth century, when cuisines began to become modernized. These cuisines have impacted what we eat in North America and in Canada.

While factors such as climate, trade, and religion have had major impacts on local cuisines, the search for the source of spices and other resources led people on expeditions to India and, by accident, the Americas. To feed European demand for sugar, plantations were established in the Caribbean, increasing demand for slave labour from Africa. Modern cuisine includes more spices, sugars, and sauces, but less game meat. Sauces are used to intensify the flavours in modern cuisine, as opposed to covering them, whereas sugar is mostly used for desserts. Not to mention that those with greater monetary means were able to afford the price of spices and sugars, highlighting social divides.

The way we associate ourselves with food has a lot to do with the environment in which we are brought up, and our diets have their own influence on our beliefs. Some food becomes central to our diets, mainly because certain dishes have a spiritual meaning. However, we also eat things that satisfy our stomachs, our taste buds, and our emotional needs. Poutine Nation did not come about because Canadians or Quebecers saw it as part of a religious practice. No church decided that poutine was suddenly an important part of the traditions and culture they propounded. In fact, poutine could be viewed as a rebellious response to an era in which the Church was influential in Quebec. Poutine, for many, has become part of rituals and represents something beyond the three main ingredients. There is something about the dish itself that connects us all in some cosmic way. It appears these days that everyone has a story related to poutine, whether they have tried it, liked it, or not. Food may be one of the most powerful, unifying, and peaceful forces humanity has had. It brings people together, allows humans to understand one another, without words, weapons, or violence. This is certainly true of poutine and what makes it such a beautiful thing.

Agriculture and Textiles

At this point, it is important to say something about the economic context in Eastern Quebec. In the nineteenth century, the economy in rural Quebec and the Eastern Townships, where I'm from, were based on two significant industries. Agriculture, of course, was one. Dairy industry innovations created poutine's cheese curds. Potatoes, corn, grains, pigs, and cattle were also critical for many rural economies in Quebec in the twentieth century. But the other industry that allowed many cities and smaller towns to prosper economically was textiles, providing a source of reliable employment and growth.[9]

One of the oldest industries in the country, the Canadian textile and clothing industry has existed for more than 150 years. Textiles were originally made from natural fibres. There was little to no machinery, and the workers were poorly trained and badly paid. This has all changed. The industry is now found in both urban and rural areas, using high-tech equipment requiring qualified personnel and producing a multitude of products. Most of us have forgotten how the industry kept towns vibrant. Even in Farnham, my hometown, the textile industry was an important sector. However, by the time I was born, textiles were on their way out.[10]

In the middle of the nineteenth century, the first textile companies were started up in Canada, and most were in the province of Quebec. The prime minister, Sir John A. Macdonald, made the textile industry a national priority. During this period, the textile industry was a major factor in the economic development of Quebec and the rest of Canada. In the Eastern Townships and southern Quebec, textiles were key,[11] and mills were the real hubs of local economies, connected by both rivers and train lines.[12]

Quebec's textile industry contributed to its urbanization and was an important element of economic development. It was, without question, a major employer in Quebec and in its rural regions. Gradually, though, price wars, foreign competition from the United States, the increasingly ephemeral life cycle of clothing, and the lack of skilled labour in the production of the raw materials for textiles brought an end to our industry. We see the beginning of the decline at the end of the Industrial Revolution in the 1950s. Many jobs were lost. These jobs kept restaurants and the service industry in small towns very busy. The other key is that these were higher-paying jobs. Not everyone could afford to go out and eat at a restaurant daily, but salaries in the textile industry made it possible. Ownership and management were dominated by English-speaking investors and individuals coming from other parts of the world. The workers, however, were all French speakers and trying to make ends meet. In Quebec, the cultural divide between the "English-speaking" executives and the French-speaking workers was obvious. Managers kept to themselves and socialized separately, and workers lived in towns and connected with each other regularly.

Poutine came along at a time when the market was ready for a new product. Life in small towns can be boring. The internet hadn't been invented, television was just beginning, and people were always looking for some form of entertainment. In those days, to get news, you read newspapers, listened to the radio, went to church, or went to town to meet people. Restaurants played an important role in gathering people who wanted to keep abreast of the latest news.[13] People visiting from other towns would meet in cafés and restaurants as places to share information, gossip, and debate politics.

In those days, serving food was an excuse to get people together, to share, and to talk. The focus wasn't the food per se. It was about facilitating a meeting place. Most small towns in Quebec and Canada had these little restaurants. They were places for workers to vent about management and other problems they were facing.[14] It was also a great place to meet a future spouse, as the textile industry employed a lot of women.

Restaurants provided a safe place for people to interact, a place where everyone was equal. Quebec is known as an egalitarian state. Remember, this was during the "years of great darkness" under Maurice Duplessis. It's not surprising that poutine was born as a result of customers asking for something that did not exist, that was not on the menu. Pioneering in food in those days was about creating something new, provided customers endorsed it.

The Industrial Revolution, Fast Food, and the Death of Cooking

Poutine was created when everything was changing politically and socially in Quebec. Our habits, our lifestyles, and many other aspects of our lives were affected by the Industrial Revolution. Cities in the nineteenth century began to grow exponentially, increasing demand for food. Not only that, as people became busier in their working lives, there was a new demand for ready-made or takeout items like pizza, hamburgers, hot dogs, and fish and chips.[15] As such items became more accessible, cooking became less central to many peoples' lives, and there was a profound impact on our relationship with food.[16] Restaurants became part of our daily lives at the time, and their influence has continued to grow in importance. Although not particularly nutritionally balanced, this diet was valued and influential.[17] After World War II, culinary changes accelerated and brought new options to what was offered in restaurants and in grocery stores. In those days, we saw the appearance of some local cuisines, and several national cuisines like French and Italian expanded. Eating outside the home became more common and has remained so in the ensuing years. The average family in Canada spends roughly 35 per cent of its budget on food cooked and consumed outside of the home, and that percentage is increasing every year.[18]

The globalization of commodities such as grains, seafood, milk, fruit, and vegetables has made many products available to a greater number of markets. But this movement has also generated some reactions against globalization. For instance, counter-cuisines like the slow food movement and locally based diets offer an alternative to this globalized view of food.[19]

Women's changing role in economic development has also played a part in how we manage meals and food in our lives. With women entering the workforce, the "traditional" female roles such as housekeeping, child-rearing, and cooking have changed. Today, everyone in the family plays a role in the kitchen, preparing food at home. The best way to manage your nutrition is to cook and prepare food at home. Yet something is happening to the importance and the sizes of our kitchens.

The Shrinking Kitchen

In many homes, the kitchen is an almost sacred place. This has been the case for a long time. As I've written elsewhere, in recent times, it appears that kitchens are "losing their lustre. An increasing number of condos and apartments are being sold and rented without a stove."[20] We see this happening more often in cities such as Toronto, Vancouver, and Montreal. "It is also happening in the United States and Europe.[21] For a growing number of households, the kitchen is more of a simple quasi-closet where you store food instead of a gathering place for family and friends."[22] This is having a profound impact on what, where, and with whom we eat.

> Since the last great recession in 2008, access to home-ownership has been a challenge, particularly for the younger generations. With rock-bottom interest rates, real estate prices have skyrocketed, making it difficult for new workers to settle and purchase a home. As such, builders are shrinking condos to keep prices at affordable levels – and the one thing that appears to be shrinking faster than ice cubes in hot soup is the kitchen. Builders know that potential buyers or renters are not going to spend much time there. Or at least, that kitchens serve a very different purpose for the younger crowd.
>
> Younger workers have a different sense of how real estate serves them. Like in many parts of the world where real estate prices have always been high, a home is a space for the in-betweens. Our busy lifestyles cause us to spend less time at home, whether it be for work, leisure, or anything else. It's a place you visit between activities. Even for people who work from home, travelling is very much part of what they do. We are slowly moving toward an app-driven food economy. Food-delivery apps are becoming the new norm.[23]

Consequently, preparing meals at home is increasingly rare.

Younger people, particularly millennials and Gen Zers, have increased demands on their time and are, therefore, three times more likely to order in than members of the baby boomer generation.[24] "A recent UBS report suggested that the global online food ordering market could grow more than tenfold over the next decade or so";[25] the food-delivery market will grow from $35 billion to $365 billion by 2030.[26] This number includes food-delivery apps often used by restaurants, prepared meal kits, takeaway ordering, and online grocery shopping. "Having food delivered will cost more but paying a premium for convenience is much less expensive than buying a full-sized condo with a kitchen you won't use."[27]

> The food service industry is also adapting to this trend. The rise of "dark kitchens" is making the industry more app-friendly.[28] These cramped restaurants, typically with no dining room and usually located in downtown cores, harbour cooks who prepare meals for food-delivery apps. They are not easy to find, but they are in most Canadian cities. In Europe and part of the United States, these dark kitchens use robotics and AI to manage orders and prepare meals, significantly reducing costs.[29] With drones and highly sophisticated delivery options, costs will likely decrease even more, making home cooking the more expensive option, especially for people living alone. With these technologies, ordering in is slowly becoming a more cost-effective dietary choice. That is the one feature that can make home cooking less attractive to everyone, not just the younger generations. Why bother cooking when it means a household generates more food waste and spends more on food?

> The economics of cooking are changing fast, which is why most grocers are investing in food service, whether it's meal kits or the ready-to-eat space. Grocers are essentially accepting the fact that consumers want to spend less time in the kitchen. As much as some of us won't want to admit this, it is happening. Cooking is being outsourced by a growing number of households.
>
> The kitchen stove could be the next sewing machine. Years ago, most homes had a sewing machine, but clothing is cheaper today than it was twenty years ago, in constant dollars. Most of us buy clothing made by someone else. The same trend seems to be happening with food. Sewing is now considered a lost art.[30]

Cooking could become one as well.

From 1957 to now, so many things have changed – how we view religion, work, consumer trends, the role of women, everything. Poutine underwent changes of its own, especially in terms of its popular status. Over time, it has become a staple of the fast-food scene and a must-have on many menus.

From Poutine Prohibition to Adulation

From a health perspective, at least, it is worth considering where poutine stands today and where it may be going in future. The trend toward healthy foods is certainly not helping poutine's popularity. Many documentaries, books, and reports suggest that we should stay away from fast food as much as we can. Poutine is part of the unhealthy food category that nutritionists and health professionals warn us against. It is filled with fat and salt, which your body doesn't need much of. Virtually everyone these days knows the risks of an unhealthy diet and that surely includes eating poutine.[31]

It could be argued that street foods and food carts, in some sense, were the beginning of the fast-food chains. What we think of today as "street food" has existed, in various forms and cultures, for centuries.[32] The major difference between street food/food carts and fast-food restaurants is that the latter are, in most cases, industrialized, with prompt customer service, an attention to safety standards, and even an assembly line approach. It is fitting, then, that fast food largely emerged from American culture before spreading all over the world. The rise of fast-food restaurants has affected how food is handled, sold, and consumed in many countries.

Many comparisons have been made between tobacco and fast food. However, it seems safe to say at this point that, in moderation, fast food is neither as harmful nor as addictive as tobacco.[33] Nevertheless, we now know that fast-food consumption is linked to obesity, cardiovascular disease, and diabetes and it is considered the leading cause of preventable death.[34] Criticism of fast food and junk food in general is linked to the way distributors market their products to appeal to young children. Marketing includes the location of fast-food restaurants close to schools.[35] Living near a concentration of "fast food restaurants has been found to be associated with a lower likelihood of eating the recommended daily intake of fruits and vegetables."[36]

Research indicates that children who live in a close proximity to fast-food outlets eat fewer fruits and vegetables, consume more sugary soft drinks, and have a higher risk of being overweight.[37]

The list of reports and studies is endless, and the consensus is clear. Fast food is bad for us, full stop. Messages like these have been conveyed to the broader public for years now, and behaviours are slowly changing. Many health professionals argue that food is medicine and that we should stay away from fast food altogether. Looking at the research, it is hard to deny this.

The criticism does not stop at the health impacts of fast food. Our obsession with fast food and junk food is to the detriment of our environment, say some critics.[38] A 2018 study suggests that most of the garbage we find in waterways, parks, and public spaces is from food companies and fast-food restaurants.[39] Companies targeted by the study were McDonald's, PepsiCo, Coca-Cola, Tim Hortons, and Nestlé.

The press has also not been kind to the fast-food industry and for decades has predicted its downfall. Yet the sector is resilient. McDonald's and many others are adjusting and continue to do well financially. Of course, the restaurant business is very competitive and challenging. Restaurants open and close regularly, yet the fast-food sector has seen record sales, a trend that seems to be continuing.

Coming back to poutine specifically, despite what is known about its nutritional value (or lack thereof), the dish is increasingly popular around the world and has even gained a kind of respect. This is interesting to see and take note of, given that, from its beginnings, poutine has been the source of some embarrassment stemming from its connection to Quebec stereotypes. As Fabien-Ouellet notes, poutine reinforces the view of Quebecers as "hewers of wood and drawers of water."[40] Yet, poutine is now known and sought out all over the world, by regular people and foodies alike.

Still, it is hard to ignore the pressing issues of record levels of childhood obesity in North America. While rates appear to have plateaued in the last decade, much work remains. This book is not meant to showcase poutine's contribution to our obesity challenges, but rather to see its role in a greater dietary context.

Policies have been implemented to make poutine, and other unhealthy foods, less accessible to children and teenagers while attending school. In 2005, junk food – and this includes poutine – was banned from school cafeterias in Quebec. It was, however, offered as a special one day per week. Even though the dish is full of salt and fat, kids continue to line up in the cafeteria on that one day to buy a poutine for lunch. When I was growing up in Farnham, as soon as winter ended, many of us walked about a mile to L'Ami du Passant to get poutine. We would make it back just in time for afternoon classes. I remember how the cheese curds would go at the bottom and on top of the fries, the way it should be. This is a great memory for me now, and it is strange to think that the dish we all craved as kids has become a symbol of bad eating habits.

It is worth noting that, unlike many fast-food items that are associated with a particular mealtime, poutine can be a snack as well, and this creates more opportunities for those who seek to market it. It also isn't a specialty item like a birthday cake or a turkey, things that are sold for special occasions and holidays. Poutine can be consumed anywhere, anytime, including after a night on the town.

Poutine is not the first so-called junk food to see a rise in status over time. Lobsters were once seen as the cockroaches of the sea and used as agricultural fertilizers in Atlantic Canada. Today, they are viewed as a delicacy, and people are willing to pay top dollar for them. In certain cases, broader societal changes and changes in tastes have taken the stigma from particular dishes or ingredients. Poutine is an excellent case in point.

CHAPTER SEVEN

What Makes a Food Trend?

History is a valuable discipline, allowing us to learn from the past, avoid repeating old mistakes, and prosper in the future. History needs to be recorded so we can remember the past, despite the difficulty of capturing a time accurately. History certainly has its flaws, but it helps us to understand who we are, where we come from, and where we are going.

Culinary history began to emerge as a distinct academic field in the 1970s. The history of food looks at everything from ingredients to equipment, presentation, eating rituals, and the meanings attached to each. The history of food is interdisciplinary and draws connections between the sciences and the humanities to encompass production, sale and distribution, preparation, and serving. Ultimately, culinary history helps us understand how food practices define community, class, race, and social status.

Fast food has attracted a lot of attention in recent years. Books such as *Fast Food Nation, Fast Food Genocide,* and *Salt Sugar Fat* or the documentaries *Where to Invade Next* and *Super Size Me* examine our bad eating habits. While many people express their reluctance to eat at a McDonald's, for example, the speed and convenience of fast food make it difficult for some to avoid, especially those constantly on the go. Let's face it, going to a restaurant or chip wagon to grab a poutine is extremely easy compared to the time it takes to prepare a meal.

In the fast-food economy, family size appears to be a significant factor in food history. With many children, families tend to spend more time in the kitchen, cooking and eating. With fewer children, social interaction around food does not occupy families as much. Since around 2005, decreasing fertility rates and increasing divorce rates have led to smaller households in the Western world.[1] Working overtime reduces the amount of time spent cooking and preparing food as well as the time families spend eating together. Studies have also shown that "the level of social interaction at the dinner table may also be lower in smaller families,"[2] which may not prioritize discussions about daily experiences. Some smaller families are also "outsourcing" home-based food production for economic reasons. The overall costs of home consumption are lower in families with few income earners and many dependents. Eating outside the household is expensive for large families.

A more educated society can also influence trends. When people spend more time in school, they have less time to cook and opt for quick solutions. They also tend to travel more. Travelling outside one's region and country exposes us to different foods, which gives local food trends a chance to become more globalized. Food trends are also linked to higher education levels and with women working full-time. These trends have made fast food a more popular option for many people.[3]

We must also bear in mind the rise of urbanization, which has accelerated in the past several decades at an unprecedented pace. "In 2014, for the first time in history, more people lived in urban areas than in rural areas" around the world.[4] This means that fewer people need cars, have higher salaries, have professional lives, and have less time to spend with their families.[5] The urban sprawl that is affecting the entire globe has increased the urban/rural divide. Rural regions, where so much of the agricultural industry is located, are now far less influential, both economically and politically, than they once were.

Urbanization is not new, of course. What is new is the rate at which it is increasing, and the societal and environmental challenges that such an urbanized population and economy create.[6] Many urbanites have little awareness of where their food comes from, which causes farmers and people living in rural regions to feel more disenfranchised, and "although cities are fuelled by diversity and entrepreneurial dynamism, they also remain the loci of major political conflicts driven by racial and cultural tensions," which are, in turn, galvanized by social media.[7] But what is often forgotten are rural communities. Or, rural communities are understood through urban values,[8] such as sustainability and animal welfare.

For many years, food trends were propelled by taste, price, availability, fashion, and aspects that may have represented underlying issues but were not explicit. In modern society, trends have meaningful depth. Perhaps it is because the food industry has seen some interesting innovations in recent years. With the rise of new generations who look at food systems differently and are expecting different things, there is added pressure on the industry to innovate – not just in terms of product offerings, but also in how food is produced, sourced, labelled, and communicated. These consumers prioritize transparency, sustainability, and ethical practices, pushing companies to rethink everything from supply chains to marketing strategies.

Of course, food trends require available ingredients. Corn, strawberries, blueberries, celery, all will become more fashionable at some point, for one reason or another. Despite the efforts of the agriculture sector, it is urban populations that dictate trends and make one commodity more fashionable than another. For instance, celery became suddenly fashionable in 2019 when Anthony Williams recommended celery juice as a means for recovering one's health.[9] This rise in popularity caused celery prices to skyrocket.[10]

While celery juice cannot be said to have persisted as a popular item for many people, poutine has weathered abrupt cycles and trend changes. Despite its rural origins, it continues to "ride the wave" of urbanization. Cheese and potatoes are mainstays everywhere. The sauce may have been an afterthought, but it was a very important afterthought nevertheless. Poutine continues to cut through the rural/urban divide, which makes it something of a miracle of Canadian culinary arts.

There is some debate about poutine emerging as a sort of accident, but we know from history that nothing is purely coincidental. Poutine is a relatively new dish and perhaps can be considered by some as a simple cultural and social phenomenon, but not a dish. This may explain why few have given poutine any attention, especially from a scientific perspective.[11]

Food history is never static – it evolves constantly, shaped by climate, political upheavals, economic conditions, and cultural transformations. At times, people respond to disruptions they themselves have caused; at others, they adapt to circumstances beyond their control. Major events – from wars and recessions to migration and technological change – leave an imprint on what we eat and how we eat it. Poutine's rise, for example, is not the story of elite chefs or corporate innovation, but of humble ingenuity. Many of the individuals behind its popularity came from large, working-class families in rural Quebec, where resourcefulness was born of necessity. In such contexts, preserving history isn't the priority – survival is. Yet out of that struggle, culinary icons emerge.

A Social Phenomenon, Food Traditions, and Poutine

I would argue that, when it comes to poutine, we need a new perspective in order to fully appreciate it as a dish and as a social phenomenon. In many ways, poutine is significant both in terms of its history and for what it says about Quebec and other parts of the world where it has been embraced.

In my view, the most compelling works of food history are those that consider multiple stakeholders and the influence of broader policies. That, at its core, is what culinary history should be – an exploration of how food connects people across every level of the supply chain, from farm to fork. Yet, in truth, much past food scholarship has been narrowly focused, often reflecting the interests of white, educated, urban professionals. This has encouraged popular writers to pursue these interests, which often only look at one aspect of food systems. This is likely why poutine or fast food hasn't received much serious, sustained study by scholars of food history.

As Matt Garcia argues, if food history is to flourish, it must "embrace interdisciplinarity and complexity, and resist simplistic interpretations of the food systems that promote only local ways of eating and that perpetuate exclusivity and class and racial boundaries."[12] Such a view may explain why poutine has been disregarded for such a long time. Most people interested in researching or reading about food focus on sophisticated dishes.[13] But issues such as race, class, gender, colonialism, and immigration are critical to understanding the not-so-glamorous facets of food systems.[14]

Since the 1990s, trends in how food is consumed in Western countries have changed deeply "due to the continuous innovation of the agro-food system and the modern evolution of lifestyles and diets, including therefore the needs of consumers."[15] This trend has involved several traditional products in America (such as hominy grits and bagels and lox) but not necessarily in Canada. Very few products that have ventured outside of Canada have been innovative. Canola is likely the most well-known Canadian export, along with maple syrup. We are also known for our beef and pork, but so are many other countries. It rings even more true when considering traditional food dishes coming from Canada. Very few people outside of Canada would know what saskatoon berry pie or Nanaimo bars are.

A traditional food product or dish is defined as follows: "a product frequently consumed or associated with specific celebrations and/or seasons, normally transmitted from one generation to another, made accurately in a specific way according to gastronomic heritage … distinguished and known because of its sensory properties and associated with a certain local area, region or country."[16] This definition is quite fitting for poutine. The main ingredients of poutine can be found anywhere in the world, but the combination is unique.

Poutine can be considered a complex Canadian product as it comes in so many different varieties. In a way, poutine is like pizza, with fries, gravy, and cheese curds acting as the dough and a seemingly limitless number of options as the toppings.

While poutine's market is well-established, nobody really knows the extent of sales on an annual basis. Canada is arguably the largest consumer of poutine in the world, followed by the Unites States. But data is difficult to obtain. Although overall food consumption is rising, consumer preferences are increasingly shifting toward eating outside the home.

This trend has fuelled the growth of fast-food chains, snack joints, and office cafeterias. As a result, market demand for ready-made and convenience foods has surged.[17]

Therefore, the poutine market is gradually evolving, even though it is quite difficult to eat a poutine while walking or driving. At the same time, there is "competition from different distribution chains [takeout, portable foods, and a large retail sector], whose growth is directly correlated to the development of different patterns of consumption,"[18] the "grocerant." As I've written elsewhere,[19] the new coinage combines "grocery" and "restaurant" and has been around for a decade or so, but it seems to have caught on only recently. The term 'grocerant' is actually very fitting and effectively reflects current trends in the food industry. The grocerant approach is as disruptive as the drive-through phenomenon was several decades ago.

> In Canada, while the numbers are [a] little more obscure, we are seeing similar trends. Many retailers are on the move. Given that convenience appears to have more currency than ever before, two worlds are currently colliding in the ready-to-eat space at grocery stores ...
>
> Grocerants offer a one-stop shopping solution for consumers driven by either curiosity or a lack of time. An increasing number of grocery stores allow customers to buy and eat on the spot, [and some facilities] merge both food retailing and food service under one roof.
>
> Research suggests many consumers generally perceive grab-and-go food products to be healthier than meals you can get at a restaurant.[20] This works well for grocers.[21]

Some say this merging in food retailing is mainly to do with the preferences of millennials and Gen Zers. It seems safe to say that it is largely in response to the demand for fresh, healthy, reasonably priced products, which is undoubtedly a priority for the younger generations that are poised to take over the economy. The changes are more deep rooted, however. Millennials and Gen Zers "have the economic influence to trigger the changes we are seeing, but many demographics are mutating and behaving differently about food. Families with older children don't mind the enhanced experienced while aging Boomers need the convenience.... The rise of the grocerant represents the awakening of an industry"[22] and is a sign of the collision of food retail and service. This trend is also self-reinforcing: As food companies merge and consolidate, the range of options available to consumers expands, which in turn shapes and amplifies consumer demand. It is also mutually reinforcing, with the merging we see, and the options available to consumers influencing demand.

I have never worked in a restaurant or a canteen myself, but my wife, Janèle, once worked at McDonald's and at the iconic Rôtisserie St-Hubert when she was young. From this experience, she learned a great deal about work, but not much about food. Her interest was in making sure that she provided good service to the patrons and was able to pay her bills. While I never worked in a restaurant myself, my first job was farming, which has a close, if somewhat different, relationship to the larger food industry.

I remember being thirteen and walking to town to be picked up by some farmers to work in the field picking strawberries all day. On the first day, there were at least a dozen kids, if not more. By the end of the day, myself and another boy, Brian Pearson, did the most work. We had picked about ten crates of strawberries, good enough to earn roughly eight dollars in one day. It was a lot of money for me in those days. Brian and I were asked to come back the next day. The farmer came to get us at our homes instead of us going to meet him in town. That's when I knew I had made the cut and earned the trust of the farmer. At the end of the season, I had earned over eight hundred dollars, enough to buy myself a Walkman and a new bike.

The restaurant business is not easy. Anyone who has worked in a kitchen or behind a bar understands the relentless pace, the long hours, and the constant pressure to deliver. It's a demanding environment where physical endurance, emotional resilience, and sharp coordination are essential. But beyond the intensity of service, the economics of owning and operating a restaurant are equally, if not more, challenging. Rising food costs, labour shortages, tight margins, unpredictable demand, and regulatory hurdles all make profitability elusive. Many restaurateurs invest their life savings and take on substantial debt just to get started. And despite their best efforts, about 80 per cent of restaurants fail within the first five years. Success in this industry is as much about grit and adaptability as it is about culinary skill,[23] which includes franchises. For a great many people, though – including many people who immigrate to Canada – these jobs can be a godsend and an opportunity to become part of a community. They are ready to work long hours under stressful conditions to give themselves a chance at a new life. In this way, food is the gateway to a new world for many people.

Poutine is very much a part of this. The origins of the dish may not be widely known but, nevertheless, it is sold throughout Canada and in many parts of the United States. It is available in restaurants as well as food trucks and carts. Even if the owners, operators, and employees have no idea where poutine came from, they know they can make a living from selling it. That awareness is a key source of confidence and hope for people, and it should never be underestimated.

PART III

The Invention and Spread

CHAPTER EIGHT

Creators, Ambassadors, and Franchises

As this book is as much about the origins of poutine as it is about its international reputation, it is hard to avoid the controversy around who invented poutine. I cannot guarantee a definitive account here. All I can do is present the information I have found and let you decide for yourself. We cannot ignore the fact that poutine is known today because of the collective work of many people here in Canada and around the world. While some authors and papers before me have credited one person or another for the creation of poutine, it would be foolish to believe that only one person is behind poutine's success. Most of the world's most famous foods came about through a collaborative and organic process, and poutine is no exception.

The Facts

It is generally agreed that poutine was created in 1957 "when a trucker [Jean-Guy Lainesse (Eddy)] asked Fernand Lachance to add cheese curds to his fries in Warwick, Quebec."[1] Lachance, who passed away in 2004 at the age of 86, was the owner of L'Idéal, a restaurant later renamed Le Lutin Qui Rit, or "The Laughing Elf." Apparently, Lainesse was in a rush and asked Lachance to add cheese to his fries and mix everything together. Lachance remarked that it was going to make a mess, a "poutine." Gravy, however, was not introduced to the poutine until 1964.

Jean-Paul Roy is credited with creating the three-ingredient poutine that we know today. His restaurant, Le Roy Jucep, in Drummondville, was the first to add poutine to its menu. It was first called *fromage-patate-sauce* (cheese-potato-gravy). Jean-Paul Roy, who passed away on August 16, 2007, at the age seventy-four, maintained that it was he who invented poutine. According to him, he began serving fries in a special sauce in 1958, which he called *patate-sauce*. His customers were adding cheese curds, sold on the side, so he added the dish to his regular menu and called it fromage-patate-sauce.[2] As the gravy tended to make the containers soggy, Roy went to Toronto to find the appropriate container to serve the dish.

Some Acadians believe tourists from the province of Quebec came up with the idea from visiting a restaurant near Parlee Beach, close to Shediac in New Brunswick, long before 1957. To date, there is no evidence to support this claim. While there are other claims, Warwick and

Drummondville have hard evidence to support their claims to being the birthplace of poutine.

The fact that cheese curds were added to fries in Warwick and Drummondville may not be a coincidence. Both are towns in which dairy farming is prominent. Warwick is widely known as the fine cheese capital of Quebec and has a rich history of producing one of the best cheeses in the country, perhaps in the world. Up until 2014, Le Festival des Fromages de Warwick (the Warwick Cheese Festival) was held. In 2014, the festival moved to Victoriaville, a much larger city about eighteen kilometres away. Unfortunately, the festival was cancelled a few years later. Warwick, Quebec, is home to Fromage Warwick, a cheese producer specializing in cheddar and cheese curds made from the milk of their Jersey cows. In Drummondville, another city heavily influenced by the dairy sector, Roy added cheese, sauce, and voilà![3] People in these two towns saw cheese everywhere, so why not on fries?[4]

The dish grew in popularity throughout rural towns in southeastern Quebec, and in 1969 it landed in Quebec City.[5] Chez Ashton, a well-known restaurant chain in Quebec City, has built its reputation on poutine. Poutine arrived in Montreal in 1983.[6] In those days, poutine was mainly associated with small fast-food outlets and food trucks. Most small towns in Quebec, and, indeed, in the rest of Canada, have something similar to *shack à patates*, small owner-operator restaurants selling fries.[7]

Most people who have started one of these businesses were former farmers, who were used to hard work and long days. In fact, working in a restaurant appeared to be less work than working on a farm.[8] These canteens were places where people gathered after church, perhaps second in popularity to the local tavern. And even then, the men would gather at the canteen after the tavern. In fact, my grandfather, Roland Charlebois, who was chief of police in Melocheville, Quebec, used to take drunk people to sober up at the local canteen. In rural Quebec, life was simple, but it could also be hard. These canteens survived by catering to people who wanted a break from their daily routine.

As poutine's market spread beyond its Quebec origins, so did the creativity of those preparing it. Cooks and chefs across Canada and beyond began experimenting with a wide range of toppings and ingredients, transforming the humble trio of fries, cheese curds, and gravy into a versatile canvas. Sausage, spaghetti sauce, pulled pork, butter chicken, smoked meat, and even lobster began appearing on menus as poutine toppings, each reflecting regional tastes or cultural influences. These variations not only showcased culinary innovation but also helped solidify poutine's status as a dynamic, evolving symbol of Canadian comfort food.

In the 1980s, poutine began to appear on the menus of various restaurant franchises. Many believed poutine was first adopted by McDonald's, but this is not the case. A restaurant chain called Frits was the first to sell poutine in 1985, but it dissolved in 1988. The spread of poutine really began in 1987,[9] when "Jean-Louis Roy, a Quebec-based Burger King franchisee, convinced the chain [Frits] to offer poutine on its menu. The dish proved so successful that the chain began selling poutine in all of its Quebec outlets, and in Hawkesbury, Ontario, the following year."[10] McDonald's copied Burger King in 1990 and was the first to sell poutine from coast to coast. Other Canadian chains such as Harvey's and A&W followed a few years later. These major franchises helped poutine gain its notoriety in a very subtle but effective way. The unassuming dish started to become popular as word of mouth spread among friends, family, and colleagues.

La Banquise (now owned by Ashton Restaurants), a restaurant located in a hip borough called Le Plateau, has made significant contributions to poutine on the Island of Montreal.[11] La Banquise was opened in 1968 by Pierre Barsalou, a firefighter, but it didn't serve poutine until the early 1980s, starting with two kinds of poutine.[12] Today, it serves well over thirty varieties. La Banquise made poutine a popular dish for trend seekers and celebrity chefs, such as the late Anthony Bourdain, who even talked about La Banquise during one of his shows.[13] Major American fast-food chains also approved poutine's entry into major markets in Quebec and elsewhere, at the same time that Le Banquise was making its mark on the island.

Poutine became a popular snack after a night on the town and was generally viewed as junk food. But then came the comfort food revolution of the '00s. Fine cuisine discovered poutine and celebrated chefs ventured to do something unique with the dish. Cookbooks were published to celebrate poutine.[14] Nowadays, it isn't just late-night revellers in Canadian cities who seek out poutine after a night of drinking.[15] Tourists visiting Canada are encouraged to try poutine at least once while visiting the country. Some tours purposely stop at a particular restaurant in order to give tourists the chance to try it. In the grand scheme of things, the rise of poutine has been incredibly fast. Within three to four decades, poutine went from being a junk-food accident to a staple on many restaurants' menus around the world, whether in the United States, Europe, Asia, or Australia.

History has shown us that innovating and creating new products does not solely happen in big cities.[16] In the case of poutine, rural communities played a huge role. Poutine would not have survived and thrived the way it has without champions who believed it might appeal to people more broadly. As hard as it is to believe now, there was a time when no one knew poutine existed outside small towns in the Bois-Francs Region. I only knew it because I was from this region. It never occurred to me that poutine was not available beyond where I lived and grew up. Food innovation is often affected by this stigma of the unknown, the inherent belief that local food traditions are not exportable.

Returning to the origins, mysteries, anecdotes, and peculiar stories that surround poutine, I can say from experience that that is how rural Quebec works. At the time, many people did not know how to write or read, hence the lack of archival evidence.[17] When living in rural Quebec, I had to write my own paycheques because many farmers could not read or write. I also recall doing it in the city, but more often in the rural communities. That's the way it was then. Things are very different today. Many farmers and people living in the country are incredibly well educated and operate highly sophisticated farms.[18]

Trying to track the invention of poutine is a bit like trying to pinpoint one person or one event that triggered the invention of beer.[19] No one really knows for sure who invented the fourth most popular drink in the world (after water, coffee, and tea), but many cultures have embraced the drink.[20] The same can be said of pizza.[21] We have some idea of who invented pizza, but nobody knows for sure. With poutine, there has been some evidence gathered over the years, which makes it relatively easy to distinguish who played a major role in the creation and commercialization of poutine.[22]

Deciding who invented poutine depends on how you define that moment, and even what constitutes a poutine. For example, the mixture of fries and cheese curds came first, and the sauce was added later. The word poutine appeared on menus much later than the dish itself.[23] The name itself, poutine, has many stories as well.[24] Like many new inventions, creating something is often a process that includes various sequential events. Sometimes, events that seem to be unrelated happen to coincide, obscuring their relationship for people in the future. Once this recognition occurs, it is then the job of the historian to try to understand how this may have happened.[25]

It's not surprising that there is disagreement over who created the famous dish. Based on the evidence, Jean-Guy Lainesse should be credited for requesting the mixture of fries and cheese curds in 1957.[26] He truly was the originator. At the time, Fernand Lachance served fries and cheese curds in a paper bag, and ketchup or vinegar were added as a side, but gravy was not included. With barbecue chicken becoming more popular in 1962, brown sauces became more popular and were offered as a side dish at Le Lutin Qui Rit.

The sauce was created by Lachance's wife, Germaine. In my mind, since the term "poutine" was coined in Warwick and all ingredients were combined for the first time at Le Lutin Qui Rit, both Mrs. and Mr. Lachance should be recognized as the "father and mother" of poutine. The word poutine appeared on a menu for the first time in Warwick. But stories in Warwick are inconsistent sometimes and not substantiated with strong evidence. For example, no dates can be found on the menu, so we don't know for sure that the menu is from the year 1957. It is difficult to credit the Lachances as the inventors, but undeniably something happened in Warwick much before Drummondville.[27] Warwick is the birthplace of the original poutine, not necessarily the modern poutine as we know it today. No authoritative evidence was ever found to prove, once and for all, that the Lachances were the inventors of poutine.[28]

Jean-Paul Roy: Inventor of Modern Poutine

Jean-Paul Roy, a trained saucier, was really the first to sell modern poutine as we know it today and should be credited as the true inventor of the dish. He valued the sauce and travelled to Toronto to find the right container to hold the three ingredients. This is likely why the Canadian Intellectual Property Office states that Roy is the inventor of modern poutine.[29] Such a recognition is hard to overlook.[30] While the Lachances should be considered as the creators of the original poutine, Roy is the inventor of the classic poutine we know and love.[31] And we cannot ignore the fact that most archives and books suggest that both Warwick and Drummondville are the most credible locations, after all these years.[32]

Creating something is not worth much unless someone champions the concept. In this light, Ashton Leblond's role is also quite critical. The way his chain embraced poutine is quite extraordinary. He gave poutine a prominent place on his menu in 1972. He believed in it and promoted it with local ingredients. Provincially, Leblond is truly the godfather of poutine.[33] His passion and dedication are unmatched. Thus I name Leblond the godfather of poutine, as he headed the first chain to promote poutine in many parts of the province of Quebec.

Nationally and internationally, the story is different.[34] Leblond passed his baton to other individuals. Chez Ashton's success is limited to the Quebec City region. Major fast-food chains, such as Burger King and McDonald's, were catalysts to poutine's popularity spreading across the country.[35] "In 1987, Quebec-based Burger King franchisee Jean-Louis Roy convinced the chain to offer poutine on its menu"[36] to compete against Chez Ashton's poutine, which was becoming more popular. He did this before McDonald's decided to add the dish to its menu.[37] Like Leblond, Roy used his foresight to recognize the dish's potential. The dish proved so successful that Burger King franchises began selling poutine across Quebec the next year, followed by most national chains. As I understand it, Roy's push to sell poutine would make him a pioneer and another godfather of poutine as a national dish.[38] These national restaurant chains propelled poutine to the sort of national and international prominence we see today, and this needs to be acknowledged in the history of the dish.

Ryan Smolkin, founder of Smoke's Poutinerie, wrote a new chapter for poutine. Smoke's Poutinerie now has franchises in the United States and plans to have over one thousand restaurants over the next few years.[39] The franchise has also expanded to the United Kingdom and the Middle East. Since 2008, the chain has aggressively promoted poutine through various international events.[40] Smolkin can arguably be credited as one of poutine's foremost ambassadors.[41]

Poutine's Godfather and Ambassadors

Most books and debates on poutine have been focused on who invented the iconic dish. What needs to be underscored is how Ashton Leblond, Ryan Smolkin, and other key ambassadors have made poutine famous. Without their work, it's unclear how poutine would have become the dish we know today.

Smoke's Poutinerie and Chez Ashton are likely the most famous examples. There are many others, but these two stories are worth looking at given how different they are. Smoke's Poutinerie is a Canadian nationwide poutine franchise founded in Ajax, Ontario. Smolkin's goal was to "bring the authentic Quebec classic to the rest of the World," according to the franchise's website. Ryan Smolkin himself was a student at Wilfrid Laurier University, which is where he got the idea of starting a restaurant chain focusing on poutine.[42] But Smolkin was in real estate and had a design

Photo 8.1. Me, in front of what is believed to be the only Smoke's Poutinerie franchise in the province of Quebec.

company before launching Smoke's Poutinerie. Smolkin has a unique background, atypical for an entrepreneur. He's an extroverted, expressive man who has made himself the spokesperson for the chain.

The first Smoke's Poutinerie opened in Toronto in 2008. Inspired by La Banquise in Montreal, Smolkin wanted to create a similar environment in English Canada. In 2008, during some time off from work following the birth of his twin sons, Smolkin uncovered a new passion when he ventured into the restaurant industry and launched his first poutinerie on Adelaide Street, near the Toronto International Film Festival headquarters at the Bell Lightbox.[43] You can't get more Toronto than that. His focus is very much on the brand. That is the key in English Canada. He sees poutine as nothing more than a mixture of three ingredients. The brand Smolkin uses is strategic, playing on the stereotype of all

Canadians being lumberjacks, wearing red and black plaid jackets, and living in cabins deep in the woods. Today, after roughly ten years, the chain has more than two hundred stores, several locations in the United States, and the recent possibility of a franchise in Qatar. It's an incredible business success. Smoke's Poutinerie is one of the first restaurant chains to have the word poutine in its name. Smolkin is the first to make poutine known to the wider world.[44] Most Quebecers have not heard much about Smoke's Poutinerie. The only restaurant in Quebec is in Mont-Tremblant, where most of the customers are from outside the province or the country. It's a smart move since the poutine market in Quebec is already quite saturated.

The recognizable face of the figurehead Smoke, a glasses-wearing man with an eighties haircut, is not based on anyone, but purely the product of Smolkin's imagination. His black and white face is everywhere, on containers, on trucks, at the front of every Smoke's restaurant. He is presented as a sort of legend, with a story about how he harvests ingredients, builds recipes, and is involved in product development. Obviously, none of this is true. From a marketing perspective, however, it is quite fascinating.

So far, Smolkin and the company have amassed several awards, such as the Pinnacle Award for Company of the Year from Food Service & Hospitality Magazine, the Hospitality Award for Fastest Growing Company in Canada, CFA Franchisees' Choice Designation and Award of Excellence, and most recently Strategy Magazine's 2015 Brand of the Year. It looks at poutine as a pure business opportunity to expand the reach of the humble dish.

Smoke's Poutinerie stands on the shoulders of another chain, the well-known Chez Ashton. Leblond and Smolkin do not know each other and took completely different approaches to poutine, but Leblond paved the way for Smolkin's success. One is all about the brand, while the other is focused on the product, freshness, and its use of local ingredients. Even though Chez Ashton bears Leblond's name, he prefers to be behind the scenes and has rarely given interviews throughout his fifty years as CEO of Chez Ashton.

Leblond's legacy came much before Smoke's Poutinerie's success. Chez Ashton is credited for making poutine famous in Quebec, or at least in the Quebec City region. Ashton Leblond is from the Eastern Townships, where I'm from. Known as the "King of Poutine," he had a typical upbringing for rural Quebec. He grew up on a dairy farm with seventeen siblings, two of whom died at a very young age, in Saint-François-Xavier-de-Brompton. He was named after an Irish lawyer who lived in nearby Bromptonville. Leblond knew little about the world, but he was ambitious and moved to Quebec City. Like most kids in rural Quebec, Leblond had a rough childhood and wanted out as soon as possible. He left school in grade 6, when he was thirteen. He earned a living working in a restaurant, washing dishes for about three dollars a day.

With seven hundred dollars in his pocket, Leblond put a down payment on a shack on wheels in 1969, selling for five thousand dollars, when he was twenty-one. In those days, you couldn't legally own a business before the age of twenty-one. He was twenty-one years old and fourteen days. The shack was called Roulotte Chez Laurette on Hamel Boulevard in Ancienne-Lorette, a very busy strip in Quebec City. The little shack was an old school bus. He kept the name of the business "Roulotte Chez Laurette" for a few months. He then called it "Ashton Snack Bar," and then "Chez Ashton." Calling a place "snack bar" in Quebec City was not all that uncommon, even if it was English.

In 1972, he introduced poutine to his customers. Not only did he come from the Eastern Townships where dairy farms were everywhere, but he also lived close to the birthplace of poutine itself. Leblond opted to add poutine to his menu in order to differentiate himself from the competition. But the dish never really became a best seller until much later. In fact, it took six years for poutine to take off. From 1972 to 1978, Leblond dedicated his work to making the best, most voluptuous gravy sauce for poutine. Often considered an add-on ingredient, Leblond took gravy very seriously. And given his success, it was the right call. To this day, the recipe for his company remains a well-kept secret.

He also took cheese curds seriously and, rather than put them at the base of the dish as is done in the Eastern Townships, he put them on top. He wanted people to see the cheese curds as they melted into the poutine. That change would create a standard in the industry. In most places now, cheese curds are on top of the fries.

Chez Ashton became a restaurant chain dedicated to serving poutine but was never successfully expanded beyond Quebec City. Leblond tried to expand the chain to Montreal twice, but was unsuccessful both times. The franchise has twenty-five restaurants in Quebec, all near Quebec City.

Chez Ashton has always been dedicated to the Quebec City region. Most of its ingredients come from there. For years, every day in January that temperatures fall below zero, Chez Ashton has offered a discount equal to the number of degrees below zero.[45] The coldest days bring the biggest discounts.[46] For a chilly place like Quebec City, it has become a successful campaign. In a way, the chain has tried to make winters more tolerable for everyone and make poutine a true comfort food on a cold winter's day. It's a brilliant campaign given that it's always difficult to get people out to eat at restaurants in cold weather.

Leblond's journey has been remarkable, to say the least. Fast, simple food gave him a chance for a better life in the big city. He started with nothing and has worked hard, more than sixty hours a week. At first, his school-bus shack was only open from May to October, closed for the winter, but in 1977 he built his first dining room. Throughout his career, Leblond has been consistently focused on fresh ingredients, good customer service, and seeing people return again and again. He always wanted local products, which may explain why Leblond was not always keen to expand beyond the Quebec City region. This intuitive focus has guided Leblond and made him the success he is today.

With the arrival of fast-food chains like McDonald's in 1977, many thought Chez Ashton's days were numbered. However, Leblond believed the quality and freshness of the product would make his business successful even if its products, especially poutine, were more expensive. Nothing at Ashton is frozen, unlike at McDonald's; therefore, Leblond never felt threatened by other fast-food chains as he had confidence in his products. Today, Chez Ashton employs over seven hundred people. Many former employees have gone on to become pilots, doctors, and highly respected professionals. This is a major source of pride for Leblond.

Leblond's legacy goes beyond the love of poutine. Despite his success, he has not achieved it without facing challenges. Sonia Reid wrote his biography in 2017, sharing Leblond's journey to success and human struggles along the way, such as a bad bout of depression in 2015.[47] The book reveals how the food industry can be both intense and life-changing. Leblond passionately dreamed of selling fries and poutine and was able to achieve his goal, so he urges others to focus on their dreams, too.[48]

Smolkin's path to success with poutine is obviously very different from Leblond's. Smolkin is from Ontario, not Quebec, and he was a university graduate who wanted to launch businesses, any business, rather than an uneducated former dairy farmer with a dream. Smolkin sells poutine to the world as a brand, which to Leblond would be an affront to the dish's purity. But it's not easy to argue with success. Smolkin has six times as many restaurants as Leblond has built in fifty years. Smolkin and Smoke's Poutinerie doesn't shy away from calling poutine a Canadian dish.

Smoke's Poutinerie gives poutine international exposure in a way that some may call appropriation. Selling poutine is no longer a small family business in rural Quebec limited by locally sourced ingredients. Smoke's Poutineries have given poutine to the world, and the company is running with it. It's about capital, and execution, and it's about branding features that are diametrically opposed to the dish's origins. But like everything else in life, things evolve. What's ironic is that most people in Quebec aren't exactly aware of what's going on. Or perhaps, most choose not to care since what is being served is not exactly what poutine is, in their minds.

Poutine: What's in the Name?

No matter what happened to the dish, who decided to sell it, or how many varieties exist, the term "poutine" itself has been consistent. I asked Ashton Leblond, the godfather of poutine, if he thought of changing poutine's name when he started to commercialize the dish in 1972. He said that it had never crossed his mind, not once.

Three syllables in French, that's it. "POO-tsi-neh," the affricate "tsi" followed by the final "neh." Other French speakers call it "POO-tin," with two syllables. English also sticks with two syllables, "poo-TEEN," but reverses the accent and lengthens the "e" sound. This is the pronunciation of choice in most parts of the world. In Quebec, the province is divided based on the primary language. French-speaking people say "POO-tsi-neh" and English-speaking people often say "poo-TEEN." The word poutine doesn't mean much of anything, or at least not officially.

It was in the early 1980s that most people began asking for the poutine we know today. However, the word "poutine" itself dates back a long time. "Deux moules à poutins" (two poutine moulds) was found in a will, listed in Montreal.[49] In 1916, Hector Berthelot's book called "Montréal: Le bon vieux temps" referenced "la poutine glissante," describing what we believe to be the Acadian poutine "rapée," which is very different from the poutine we know today.[50]

The word itself is shrouded in mystery. One predominant story that is often mentioned in popular culture is the 1957 story of Jean-Guy Lainesse, poutine's creator. When he was asked to mix both cheese and fries together, Fernand Lachance, the father of poutine, said that it would make a "maudite poutine," or a damn mess, as suggested by other articles. What we know is that Fernand Lachance was the first one to ever add the word "poutine" to his restaurant's menu, which he did in 1957. No artifact has ever been produced showing that the word was used for the dish before that time. Other than that, since this is based on what people may have said, my theory rests on anecdotal evidence, but it is unclear that "poutine" may mean mess.[51] According to the Merriam-Webster dictionary, a popular etymology is that poutine originates from a Québécois jargon word meaning "mess."[52] Such an interpretation, in my mind, is historical but also based on some assumptions.

There is some amusing history behind the explanation of the meaning "mess" and poutine. According to some archives, the English initially borrowed the French word "boudin" to create the word "pudding," only to see the French borrow it back to create the word "poutine." The 1988 edition of Larousse Gastronomique explains that poutine comes from the Provençal word "poutina," which means porridge.[53]

About fifty kilometres away, in Drummondville, the name has a different origin. When Jean-Paul Roy, the inventor of the modern poutine, put all of the ingredients together, he named the dish after his cook at the time. His name was Ti-Pout, short for poutine. In many parts of rural Quebec, it was common to call anyone Ti-something. Ti, from "petit," stands for short or little, but it is also used for someone who may be popular in a small town, someone who may be affectionate and friendly. Many restaurants in rural Quebec were named Ti-something to give the business a friendly, hospitable feel. It is still the case today.

Another theory is that the word poutine may have come from the English word "pudding." People in Quebec have been using the word to refer to various desserts, or puddings, since at least 1810. They both sound the same. Some say that the word poutine comes from "put in" as in "put the cheese in the fries," but that hypothesis has little support.[54] Jean-Paul Roy may have mixed both Ti-Pout with pudding to come up with the name poutine. What is unclear is how two cities, close to each other, would have come up with the same exact name in a short period of time. Coincidence? No one knows for sure.

Not only is the name poutine easy to pronounce; it is also easy to remember. Most people who hear the word poutine remember it – it sticks.[55] Under certain conditions, highly emotional words are remembered better than words invoking a lesser emotional response.[56] Poutine inspires someone to think of fun and pleasure.[57] Context often makes a word memorable.[58] Poutine, as a dish that lends itself to being shared, is, for the most part, associated with friends, family, and happiness, which makes the word poutine more memorable.

The word poutine is also used in France for another type of dish, which has nothing to do with the poutine we know in Canada. Poutine in Cagnes-sur-Mer is translucent caviar coming from sardines. It is fried and gives this dish a unique nickname: the grey gold of the Mediterranean. But it's not widely known, and new fishing regulations in Europe may prevent people from eating it altogether.[59] There is also the "poutine râpée," a traditional dish from the great region of Acadia. It is even older than Quebec's poutine and owes its origins to Germany as well as to Acadia, but it's a completely different dish. In its most common form, it consists of a boiled potato dumpling with a pork filling. It is usually prepared with a mixture of grated and mashed potato.[60] It is not like Quebec's poutine, but it is well-known in Acadia.[61]

The word poutine doesn't really have a synonym either, although some call the dish by a different name. In some parts of Quebec, like Plessisville, poutine is called "mixtes," which means a mixture of ingredients. In fact, poutine has several different names in many parts of Quebec, but the basis of the dish remains the same.

CHAPTER NINE

Poutine: Canada's Pizza

Many countries have a unique dish that establishes their culinary identity. Think of how closely Spain is associated with paella, a rice dish that includes whatever is in season. Vegetable paella typically includes ingredients like beans, peas, and onions, while meat-based versions use wild hare and venison, and seafood paella features a variety of fresh, locally caught fish and shellfish. Irish stew isn't just a staple in the country it is named for, it can be found in Irish pubs around the world. The broth is thick and made with slowly simmered mutton, onions, potatoes, carrots, and parsley. Pot-au-feu, which means pot-on-the-fire, is originally a rustic French dish made with stewing steak, root vegetables, and spices.[1] Tacos are a traditional Mexican dish consisting of a tortilla, made from either corn or flour, folded or rolled around a variety of fillings. Ackee and salt fish, originally invented by slaves forcibly brought from

Africa, is now a national food in Jamaica. Ackee, a fruit that resembles scrambled eggs, is sautéed with salt fish, along with various seasonings and aromatics. Peking Duck is China's national dish, which uses maltose syrup as a glaze for a duck that is roasted in an oven till it browns.[2] And who can forget pizza from Naples, Italy, which in its original form uses three ingredients: tomato sauce, cheese, and crust. Pizza is widely known around the world as one of Italy's most significant contributions to the culinary world.

Let's compare pizza and poutine. Both are simple to make and are easy to customize to any given market. Both can take nearly any topping and are easy to share. Pizza was invented in Italy and is now recognized worldwide. Despite certain parallels, however, both poutine and pizza have quite different histories. Can we compare poutine's international success to pizza? Is there something unique to be learned from how pizza became a standard dish? Considering pizza and poutine as historical artifacts offers an opportunity to access the hidden history found in the conventions of everyday mealtime. Furthermore, by considering pizza's origins and comparing it to poutine's, the growth of its popularity, and widespread commercialization as an ethnically identified enterprise, we also gain opportunities to better understand concepts associated with historical thinking and cultural diffusion.[3]

When you think about it, consuming food is far more than a biological necessity – it's a deeply social act that allows us to reflect on the foundational structures of a society. Every bite we take can reveal insights into power dynamics, class distinctions, gender roles, and cultural transformations. For example, the rituals surrounding who cooks, who eats first, and who serves whom often mirror broader societal values and hierarchies. Food consumption, in this sense, becomes a mirror for how power is distributed and how social norms are reinforced or challenged.

Take pizza as a case in point. Its journey from a humble Neapolitan street food to a global staple reveals broader forces of immigration, cultural exchange, and fluid national identities. Italian immigrants in North America adapted their culinary traditions to new ingredients and consumer expectations, turning pizza into a symbol of both ethnic heritage and mainstream convenience. Over time, it became one of the most democratized foods, crossing class, racial, and cultural boundaries, served everywhere from school cafeterias to artisanal wood-fired bistros.

Fast food, too, emerged from specific historical and social pressures. It was not born out of indulgence but out of necessity—a response to the growing demand for convenience in a rapidly industrializing world. The post-World War II economic boom brought with it sprawling suburban developments, an automobile-centric culture, and a shift in family dynamics, particularly with more women entering the workforce. These transformations called for quick, predictable, and portable meals. Enter the fast-food chains, drive-ins, and strip malls – architectural and commercial innovations that symbolized a new way of living.

The arrival of ready-to-eat meals, then, is not just a culinary shift – it represents a broader cultural reconfiguration. It speaks to changing family structures, time scarcity, consumerism, and even shifting definitions of home and community. In the process, food lost some of its communal and ritualistic functions but gained new roles in expressing identity, mobility, and modernity. Ultimately, what we eat, how we eat, and where we eat can reveal as much about a society as any political speech or economic policy.[4] In essence, fast food is a product of our modernized society and urbanization. That is what prompted more innovation, which created various dishes and made some more widely known, such as pizza. After World War II, the close relationship of pizza to the emergence of the fast-food outlets and takeout places in the industrialized world highlights the dramatic alterations in family life, women's roles in our economy, and the shift in the Canadian population from cities to suburbs. Poutine's story is almost the opposite. It originated in rural Canada and spread to cities, first in Canada, then to other parts of the world.

The word *pizza* can be traced back to the tenth century, with one of the earliest known references appearing in a Latin manuscript from the town of Gaeta, in what is now southern Italy. In that context, pizza referred not to the iconic dish we recognize today, but rather to a type of flatbread – likely simple, rustic, and baked in communal ovens. It was often used as a generic term for any kind of baked dough, possibly topped with herbs or cheese, but it bore little resemblance to the modern version loaded with tomato sauce, mozzarella, and various toppings.

This early pizza was likely more a reflection of subsistence food than culinary identity – a staple among the working poor. It was utilitarian and local, reflecting the ingredients available and the baking practices of the time.

The dish evolved slowly over centuries, absorbing the influences of trade, conquest, and migration.

It wasn't until the eighteenth and nineteenth centuries in Naples that pizza began to take the form we know today, especially with the introduction of tomatoes to Europe following the Columbian Exchange. Tomatoes were initially thought to be poisonous, but by the 1700s, they were being embraced by the poor in southern Italy and added to flatbreads, giving rise to the first recognizable pizzas. So while the word pizza may have ancient linguistic roots, its cultural and culinary significance only began to crystallize much later, shaped by centuries of change and adaptation.

Naples, Italy, unlike Drummondville or Warwick in Quebec, is a city of more than a million people with a nobility that frowned upon pizza as commoner food. This changed in 1889 when Margherita of Savoy, the Queen consort of Italy, ordered and took delivery of a pizza.[5] With spreading immigration, pizza spread out from Italy to take over the world.[6]

The importance of immigration in the transmission of foods cannot be understated. Throughout the late nineteenth and early twentieth centuries, many Italians migrated to the United States to start a new life. Many had simple jobs, working on the eastern seaboard of the United States.[7] In the history of pizza in North America, New York is a critical locus. In 1897, Gennaro Lombardi established the first pizzeria in Little Italy.[8] Lombardi's is often said to be the oldest pizzeria in North America. It closed in 1984 and reopened in 1994 under a new owner and at a new location in Manhattan's Little Italy.

There is likely a Little Italy in many major cities around the world. These hubs enabled pizza to prosper and brought attention to the dish outside Italy. Poutine never really benefited from such a network. Poutine's fame has grown regardless, through word of mouth, and perhaps with a little help from social media. A very different history for poutine indeed.

Like poutine today, almost everyone knows about pizza. Its three main ingredients are easily recognized, as is pizza's origin in Italy. Poutine also has three well-known ingredients, and most would know that it originated in Canada. As poutine is for Canada, pizza might be the most readily identifiable, internationally recognized Italian item in the world.

The other great similarity between pizza and poutine is that both had humble beginnings. Both now have an international reputation, and neither of the dishes was popular or well-known in the beginning. I want to emphasize this point because so many national dishes have originated in major centres where there are large numbers of people.[9] When pizza was not a recognizable dish, it was described by many as a "species of most nauseating cake that looks like a piece of bread that has been taken reeking out of the sewer."[10] Pizza was unappetizing peasant food. Today, many gourmet restaurants offer pizza as a sophisticated item on their menus. The same can be said about poutine. Poutine is unglamorous, simple, and disgusting for many. Yet poutine is now offered many ways and fits all budgets. The fact that the dish is so much better known allows people to overcome their original reluctance.

When you look at the history of both dishes, the speed with which they both gained global notoriety is quite similar.[11] Pizza took about fifty to sixty years before it became the well-known dish that it is today. Poutine took roughly the same amount of time. Both have different histories, but the human aspect of their stories is real, unique, and historical.

Poutine's demand globally may have been stimulated by travelling Canadians, but it appears many non-Canadians played an important role in making poutine famous. For pizza, at first, it was all about Italian pride, making a living and establishing a new life in the New World. Compared to such intentions, poutine became famous almost by accident, though that isn't to say that there wasn't work and passion behind it.

How Is Poutine Iconic?

At this point in the book, we have clearly established poutine's iconic status. But what makes it an icon, really? Can we say that butter tarts are iconic? Or the BeaverTail? Or could Nanaimo bars have that status as well? It is a new dish compared with England's Christmas pudding or Italy's pizza. Perhaps poutine is a product of its time – hip, simple, for the average person. Some dishes attained iconic status due to colonialism, or because they are connected to a well-known celebration, such as the Christmas pudding.[12] When visiting Wimbledon, the most prestigious tennis tournament in the world, you'll find people eating strawberries and cream. It has become a tradition with its own history.[13]

In some senses, an iconic dish defines a nation inasmuch as the nation defines the dish. According to Scholliers,[14] food practices are an important reflection of our culture and nationality. It is a mechanism with which we build our individual and collective identity.[15] To reach an iconic status, a dish also needs to become known internationally. It has happened to many dishes. Immigrants often bring along traditions, and of course, food recipes.

In the case of poutine, migration occurred through different channels and in a disorganized fashion. Military and restaurant chains added poutine to their menus, entrepreneurship and branding helped to spread the dish, and, in doing so, determined where it would most frequently be found and who ate it. Over the last forty years or so, while more and more Canadians have travelled to different parts of the world, poutine has travelled with them.

Iconic dishes rarely emerge in isolation. They are often the result of centuries of cultural exchange, adaptation, and negotiation – especially between Indigenous Peoples and colonists or settlers. Many of the world's most recognized national or regional foods carry the imprint of Indigenous ingredients, culinary techniques, and food philosophies that have shaped them in profound but often underacknowledged ways. From the use of corn, beans, and squash in North American cuisine, to the incorporation of native spices, fruits, and cooking methods in South America, Africa, and Oceania, Indigenous contributions are foundational. Settlers brought their own foodways, but they often had to adapt them using what was locally available – wild game, native grains, and traditional preservation techniques –

which led to the creation of hybrid dishes. These iconic foods, now celebrated as cultural symbols, are in many ways the edible record of Indigenous resilience, colonization, and ongoing cultural exchange. Recognizing this helps us better understand not just the food itself, but the history and identity it represents.[16] When it comes to symbolic dishes, national tradition often prevails over local circumstances. These foods take on meanings that transcend geography and reflect collective identity. For instance, poutine is served across Canada as a symbol of Québécois culture, even though its origins are deeply local and rural. Japan's sushi, once a regional food tied to coastal fishing communities, has become a global emblem of Japanese refinement and culinary precision. Italy's pasta dishes, like spaghetti bolognese, are embraced as national staples despite their regional origins – bolognese from Bologna, for example – often with variations that would surprise locals. In the United States, Thanksgiving turkey is a national tradition, regardless of regional preferences or the fact that wild turkey wasn't universally available across the country historically. These dishes become codified into national narratives, sometimes losing their local nuances in the process.

Symbolic dishes embody cultural values, express meaning, and evoke feeling, particularly during times of change or in unfamiliar settings.[17] For the English, pudding represents Christmas, family, nation, and empire. In the case of poutine, strong sentiments link the dish with meeting up and sharing with friends, nation, and tolerance. Up until now, little research has been done to fully understand what poutine means to Canadians. Tolerance is a strong Canadian sentiment that can apply to poutine. Poutine is plain and unwholesome, but we have now accepted it for its uniqueness and flaws.

As a regional dish, poutine has enabled Canadians to assert their cultural identity in a global food landscape dominated by homogenizing fast-food chains. In a world sharply divided by class and ethnicity, poutine crosses sociocultural lines and is something people enjoy anywhere.[18]

Simply put, iconic dishes become iconic for their uniqueness, their associations, and their fame outside a country. There are other well-known Canadian dishes, to be sure, like the Halifax donair or the lobster roll. Outside Canada, though, one must wonder if these are distinctly Canadian or simply part of a larger ecosystem based around certain products. Canadians also tend to glorify commodities, like corn in the summer, strawberries, or even blueberries. Many other nations produce these commodities, and they require no unique perspective or cultural knowledge. It should also be noted that iconic dishes change over time and can adapt to new settings and trends.[19] This is certainly the case with poutine, which has proven malleable across generations, though, comparatively speaking, it is a rather more recent invention.[20] Will it survive over time? No one really knows.

A Dish and Social Identity

Certain dishes, we have seen, play a significant part in the social identity of a given group or a nation. Poutine is very much that for many people in Quebec. It is impossible to visit a Canadian kiosk or tourist boutique without seeing something about poutine. Airports, fairs, tourist attractions, it's everywhere.

Younger generations in Quebec simply cannot avoid poutine and have been brought up with it as a tradition. Eating poutine is very much part of the province's social fabric, whether people outside Canada associate it with Quebec in particular or with the country as a whole.

The process by which food becomes part of a nation's social identity is not simple. It is a long journey. In the case of poutine, like pizza, it took about fifty years or so. Social identification is the product of seeing oneself as part of a social group. It involves emotion, motivation, and powerful feelings that bring one to define themself as part of a collective.[21] Social identity in food shapes behaviour and choices. You can eat a dish to signal your attachment and even perhaps follow specific social norms.[22] Research has found a direct link between social identity and the food we consume. People increase or decrease their food intake based on the behaviour of the in-group but not the out-group, indicating that group norms shape food consumption.[23] Sports fans either eat more or eat certain types of food when their team loses as opposed to when they win. Immigrants will eat local foods as they are readily available and give them a sense of fitting in.

In school, young people eat similar foods for similar reasons, often shaped by institutional norms, convenience, and cultural expectations. School cafeterias typically offer standardized meals that prioritize affordability, ease of preparation, and nutritional guidelines set by education or health authorities. As a result, students across different regions may eat items like pizza slices, chicken nuggets, sandwiches, or pasta – foods that are familiar, broadly accepted, and easy to serve in large quantities. Peer influence also plays a role: students tend to choose foods that are socially accepted or popular among their classmates. Moreover, time constraints and limited options further contribute to this uniformity. In many cases, even students who bring lunches from home gravitate toward packaged snacks, juice boxes, and simple sandwiches, reflecting broader food marketing trends and parental concerns about nutrition, cost, and convenience.

Social identity and food have little to do with actual satisfaction or how much someone likes the product or dish itself. In many cases, the connection is not about taste or enjoyment but about what the food represents. Most of this connection is internalized – shaped by upbringing, culture, family traditions, and social context. For example, someone might feel proud eating a dish associated with their heritage, even if it's not their favourite in terms of flavour. A Scottish person might eat haggis on Burns Night not because they love it, but because it symbolizes national pride and a connection to ancestry.

There is growing evidence in psychology and behavioural science that social identity can shape both the expected and the experienced pleasantness of food consumption.[24] In other words, if a dish is closely associated with one's cultural or group identity, people may anticipate liking it more – and that expectation can influence how enjoyable they actually find it when eating. Social identity can subtly – but powerfully – influence our relationship with food, often in ways that go beyond pure sensory experience.

If the group of people you are with is ordering poutine, you may follow suit, whether you want to or not. Research suggests that food choice may be influenced by the salience of a particular social identity, suggesting that the influence of social identity permeates the eating experience.[25] This may explain why some dishes become popular and transcend the locality from which they emerged, while others do not.

The motivation to self-identify may also vary. It can be about wanting to belong to a particular social group and connect in certain ways. Politics also play a significant role in the food industry in our modern era, often intertwined with the exploitation of food producers, abuse of animals, environmental destruction, serious healthcare issues, and unfair distribution that, at its worst, leads to "food deserts," food scarcity, and mass starvation. Activism and dietary choices come together more often than ever.[26] You choose to eat something because it has a certain meaning, or it represents a set of values that you want to adhere to, such as vegetarianism or veganism representing kindness to animals or concern for the environment. The clash between vegetarians/vegans and meat eaters has created a highly polarized market when it comes to food.[27]

Social identity clearly extends beyond the domain of food. It's not about taste, fashion, or exploration, necessarily. In food, there is such a thing as a right and a left wing. The food left wing has an acute interest in socio-environmental issues and human rights. The food right wing, on the other hand, has a greater interest in carrying forward food traditions and the right to hunt.[28] What is interesting is that these groups consume information differently. Social interactions between and among people on the left and on the right show segregated structures, indicating different information consumption patterns. Similar to politics, food choices are based on acquired information from sources someone trusts. Food identity may, in fact, be a proxy for personal attributes.[29] In other words, you eat meat because you believe that it makes you tough and strong. For poutine, it may be because you want to be seen as a fun, easy-going person within a larger group.

Psychology also plays a large role when choosing a dish.[30] Comfort food exists for a reason, and a big part of poutine's success may be that it falls into this popular category. In a sense, poutine avoids the kind of political pitfalls some other foods have come to be associated with.[31] It can be served to any palate, any taste, any diet, including vegetarians. This, combined with the simplicity of its design and its humble, unpretentious origins, makes poutine unique as a socio-cultural signifier.

Is Poutine Part of Canada's National Identity?

Many believe that the only thing that can change a country's image is a change in the way a country sees itself.[32] Indeed, this kind of self-image will often influence how the country promotes and brands itself abroad. Yet these concepts are also interrelated with the whole notion of national reputation. A national reputation encompasses various aspects, including a country's foreign policies, style of government, its culture, tourism, exports, and, of course, its cuisine.[33] Unlike many other factors, food is heavily influenced by corporations and the private sector's ability to promote and sell products, recipes, and dishes.

The success of so many of the iconic dishes we know today can be traced back to the early efforts of small enterprises, often humble, family-owned businesses that relied on hard work, creativity, and community support rather than large-scale marketing or industrial production. These businesses were often embedded in local neighbourhoods, serving food that reflected the traditions and tastes of their cultural heritage, while also adapting to local ingredients and customer preferences.

For example, pizza as we know it today gained widespread popularity thanks to Italian immigrant families in cities like New York and Chicago, who opened small pizzerias that introduced their regional recipes to broader audiences. Similarly, bagels became a staple in North American cities through Jewish bakeries that preserved and shared Eastern European baking traditions. Tacos, once a modest street food in Mexico, became a global phenomenon due in large part to small taquerías and family-run food trucks that brought regional variations like al pastor or carnitas to new urban markets.

Even fried chicken, often associated with Southern cuisine, owes its popularity to generations of Black-owned restaurants and informal establishments that preserved recipes passed down through families – long before fast-food chains commercialized the dish. The same can be said for butter chicken and naan, which were staples of small Indian restaurants before becoming mainstays in Western food courts and supermarkets.

In all of these cases, it was the persistence and passion of small business owners – often operating on tight margins and with limited resources – that helped define, preserve, and eventually elevate these dishes into beloved cultural icons. Their efforts laid the groundwork for what would become major food trends, influencing global palates while preserving deep local and cultural roots.[34]

Branding a nation, though, is not a simple thing, especially where food is concerned. For one thing, it can be difficult to determine what constitutes a nation as opposed to a nation-state.[35] Given the complexity of trade, immigration, language, and other related issues, defining a socially constructed "nation" can be extremely challenging as the concept itself is not clear or well defined. No nation will speak the exact same language, have all its citizens think alike, or even have everyone eat the same dishes. And even if, say, one country does speak the same language, it would not mean that a nation can be defined. Social constructs must be continually reconstructed to keep pace with reality. Nation branding is a little like nation building. It's a process that takes time and can only be planned and controlled to a certain extent.

For example, Canada hosted the International and Universal Exposition in 1967, in Montreal. Hosting the Expo was suggested by Senator Mark Drouin of Quebec, to highlight Canada's one-hundredth birthday celebrations. The overall theme of Expo '67 was "Man and His World." What was showcased at the time were dishes that reflected the history of the New World. Canada's food tent at Expo '67 featured meats such as beluga, beaver, char, and bison. These meats took centre stage in the pavilions for Canada, Quebec, Ontario, and the Atlantic Region.[36] At the time, there was no poutine to be found to represent Canada. Today, one would likely expect a very different menu based on a mixture of how we would like to be perceived and how we see ourselves as a nation.

I wasn't born when Expo '67 took place, but I did visit the 2015 World Expo in Milan, Italy, with my family. You can tell a lot about how countries see themselves by visiting pavilions from around the world.[37] Expo 2015 was the first world's fair with a food theme: "Feeding the Planet, Energy for Life." Each country was asked to offer possible solutions to hunger and food insecurity. The Expo also focused on human nutrition and nurturing our environment. Yet, while walking around the various pavilions, I noted little engagement with the problems the world food system actually faces. Canada didn't go to Expo 2015, so we were not able to see Canada's view of itself from outside its borders. I, however, would have been surprised if poutine had not been available and marketed.

Also, in time, stereotypes are widely held notions that are oversimplified beliefs and images that people hold about other nations because of their lack of knowledge about the nation itself.[38] Stereotypes can be outdated and are often overly general. Furthermore, these stereotypes are often wrong, unfair, and difficult to change.[39] When the stereotypes are wrong, at least then there are ideas to build upon when promoting a nation's image. Smolkin's approach to poutine with Smoke's Poutinerie is all about stereotypes of Canadian culture, and he makes no apologies for it. Canadian stereotypes are a source of pride for him. Stereotypes are cognitively unavoidable, whether based on nations or not. Yet, stereotypes do evolve, as they rarely represent an absolute truth. They are not a perfect representation of the world, but subject to ongoing revision and cultural (mis)communication.

As I think of poutine and how it has become so internationalized, I can't help but think how its success is influencing or may have influenced our nation's image and reputation. The increasing homogeneity in global food supplies and the implications on culinary arts and food trends allow dishes like poutine to gain more exposure. Even though the name may not be familiar, the three ingredients are very familiar to the world. There is nothing unique about potatoes, cheese curds, and gravy.[40]

Is Poutine Part of Canada's Food Identity?

It has often been said that you are what you eat. There is some truth to that. People eating poutine are not necessarily labelled one way or another but eating too much of it will eventually take its toll.[41] On a national level, what we eat influences the reputation of our country, and our values around food impact perceptions and expectations abroad.

Unlike certain countries – France and Italy come to mind – Canada is less widely known for its unique gastronomy and culinary history. Despite Canada's relative youth, its culinary fame is starting to rise.

As we have seen, food and food habits are benchmarks of culture, shaping individual and collective identities.[42] Food can allow a nation or a group to remember its past and set a new path for the future. Food is also a very powerful bordering agent. It delineates national boundaries, shaping them socially, culturally, and physically.[43] The foundation of any food identity lies in how it reflects and honours the topography of a region – its climate, soil, terrain, and natural resources. From coastal seafood traditions shaped by ocean proximity to mountainous cuisines built around hearty grains and preserved foods, the landscape directly influences what people grow, harvest, and eat. Over time, this deep connection to the land becomes more than just sustenance; it evolves into a form of cultural expression. Food becomes a way to narrate the story of a place – its rhythms, challenges, and abundance. A region's cuisine is therefore not just a collection of recipes, but a living reflection of its geography, its history, and the intimate relationship between people and their environment.[44]

Food identities are a collective phenomenon whereby individuals subject to a national political authority are alike, and distinctive in their shared food norms related to values, beliefs, symbols, myths, and agrarian traditions.[45] Of course, this does not happen overnight. Food identities are a construct and rarely develop in a straightforward fashion. The surprising rise of poutine's popularity is a great example of how this happens. While a number of people played key roles, the actual process and eventual outcome is beyond anyone's control. Which brings us to the question: Is poutine an anchor to Canada's food identity?

Central to many dishes that define a particular culinary identity is the idea of "refinement." In order to be considered part of this elite group, a dish should not be simple to make or be widely accessible. Instead, it should be rarefied, expensive, and complex.

According to traditional criteria for what constitutes an iconic national dish – such as historical depth, culinary refinement, broad regional appeal, or ties to elite gastronomy – poutine should never have risen to prominence. Originally a working-class, rural snack born in small-town Quebec, it was often dismissed as greasy, unrefined, and emblematic of lowbrow comfort food. For years, it lacked the culinary prestige or cultural cachet typically associated with national symbols. Yet poutine defied expectations. Only recently has it undergone a transformation – reinterpreted by chefs, embraced by urban food scenes, and featured in upscale dining contexts. This newfound sophistication has allowed people to reframe it not only as a legitimate expression of regional culture but as an integral part of Canada's broader food identity. In some circles, it is even regarded as a refined dish, capable of carrying gourmet ingredients and complex culinary narratives, all while preserving its humble roots.

Poutine is truly a miracle of food socialization.[46] We don't always think about the food we eat in this way, but food can be an agent of socialization, something that is culturally prescribed and has a significant influence on those who consume it. People who move to Canada, whether immigrants or international students, go through a process of adopting a new culture, and food is a critical part of this process. It is part of becoming familiar with a culture until they can establish themselves within it.[47] This two-way street of transference helps to explain why poutine has become such an important part of the culture inside Canada and why it has spread so far and fast outside its borders.

Poutine filled a perceptual void that existed around the world by offering a uniquely Canadian culinary symbol in a landscape where the country lacked a strong, internationally recognized national dish. For decades, Canada was often perceived as culturally adjacent to the United States or Europe, with little gastronomic identity of its own. Poutine changed that. Its unapologetically indulgent mix of fries, cheese curds, and gravy became an emblem of cultural authenticity – unpretentious, comforting, and unmistakably Quebecois in origin. Over time, it evolved into a canvas for culinary creativity and a point of pride for Canadians, allowing the country to project a distinct food identity that resonated globally. In doing so, poutine gave Canada a voice in the global food conversation – a role it had long lacked.

It appropriately became our pizza, or stew, our hamburger. Can any other Canadian dish replicate the same phenomenon? Possibly. But the kind of global recognition we see in the case of poutine isn't something that could have been planned. It is the collective work of many individuals and many lucky occurrences. Canada's culinary journey is only beginning, and some other dish may come along to surpass poutine, perhaps something that isn't so strongly associated with Quebec. Canada is, after all, a diverse country, comprised of people of many cultures. Whatever is showcased around the world to represent Canada must represent diversity, tolerance, and openness. We still have much to do in the kitchen to give Canada a renewed and meaningful reputation.

Poutine, as a symbol of food identity in Canada, may seem like a strange choice, given its obscure origin story and less-than-healthy nutritional value. Despite this, many people are willing to accept it. I still hope that one day other dishes may receive similar attention and prominence both inside and outside Canada.

Pride and Poutine

How much pride should Quebecers take in the success of poutine? It's complicated. After all, it is not a healthy dish, and it is not always pleasant to look at. In the hands of someone who doesn't know what they're doing, the result can be abominable. So, even if poutine has become a cultural icon, how much pride should Canadians take in it?

Canada is a rich country with abundant resources. It is also a new country, a young nation compared to many others. Most of the dishes we eat have been imported from abroad and, for many Canadians, food offers a sense of comfort and security. This isn't the case in all parts of the world. War, poverty, natural disasters, and many other things can affect a country's ability to survive. We are fortunate in Canada in that food is so often a reason to come together, something we too readily take for granted.[48]

Sometimes it is precisely such terrible challenges that cause a dish – and other cultural signifiers like art – to flourish. Food has been a sustaining force throughout history, not just in terms of nourishment but also as a powerful catalyst for social cohesion and political unity. Across different civilizations and eras, shared meals, feasts, and agricultural rituals have played central roles in bringing people together – solidifying community bonds, fostering alliances, and diffusing tensions. In ancient societies, food offerings were part of religious and diplomatic practices; in modern times, food aid has been used as a strategic tool for peacekeeping and rebuilding war-torn regions.

From the communal bread ovens of medieval villages to contemporary global initiatives like the World Food Programme, food has symbolized not just survival but solidarity. When access to food is equitable and secure, it promotes stability, reduces conflict, and helps build trust among citizens and nations alike. In this way, food acts as both a basic human right and a foundation for lasting peace – linking economies, cultures, and political agendas in the pursuit of shared prosperity.[49]

Considered contextually, food assumes a deeper, more affective role that reaches people on an emotional, psychological, even spiritual level. It happens all over the world: national dishes become rallying points for people and key to their livelihoods.[50] In fact, when you consider the history of some countries and how important food has been to their cultures, Canada can seem somewhat insignificant. There are traditions, naturally, and millions of Canadians use food to honour their heritage. We cannot overlook this fact. Still, compared to what you find elsewhere in the world, the relationship of most Canadians to the foods that they eat is less profound.[51]

While travelling through Europe, I met lots of people from different backgrounds. I was once hosted by a family in Bordeaux, in the south of France. For the first time in my life, I realized how food actually saved France, culturally. Everything around the table had a meaning. What we ate, how we ate it, with what wine, and who was invited. That's when I realized how food was trivialized in Canada. In Parma, Italy, I quickly learned that the country's regions have distinct food cultures. Events were organized around food all the time: indoors, outdoors, with families, and in the community. I recognized the same thing in China. Every time I was hosted by a group or a university, I noticed how food and drinks meant something particular within the culture, and the histories of dishes were always explained with pride. The richness of a nation's history accumulated with disputes, wars, and famine. Food became a symbol of victory, inviting people to recognize that they had conquered something significant. To the people I was visiting, nothing was more powerful than sitting down for a meal after accomplishing something grand. For example, while I was in China, a host explained to me that one of the dishes came from his ancestors' recipe, which went back eleven generations. Knowing this simple fact had such a profound impact on my relationship with the food. It was breathtaking to consider the ingredients and recipes that have been transmitted over hundreds of years.

Food alters our senses and triggers memories. It is a means through which we relate to our communities and our environment. Citizens often define themselves as part of a political system, but food can be an equally powerful signifier of identity. Descartes famously said, "I think, therefore I am." With food, we can say, "I eat certain dishes, therefore I am."[52]

Having experienced a wide range of cuisines from around the world, some of which are very refined, I can say with certainty that poutine is a unique dish and should not be judged solely by its simplicity or nutritional value (or lack thereof). I feel strongly that poutine embodies many of Canada's values as a nation, among them tolerance, friendship, sharing, and diversity. Like so many famous dishes, poutine has its traditions. But these are young traditions, and there is still time for the dish to develop and transform in interesting ways. In a metaphorical sense, this is very much like Canada itself, something young, rich in diversity, and full of potential.

As Canadians, we aren't as quick to express our pride as the citizens of certain other countries. We should feel proud, though, when we look at the success poutine has had, and how, against the odds, it has become a true icon. Canada and Quebec should embrace this unique and quirky contribution to the rest of the world and let it evolve in different ways, in different places. It is rare to find a dish that outlives trends and cycles as poutine appears to be doing.[53]

Some Quebecers believe the world should adopt the dish as it is, as tradition dictates. As poutine becomes internationalized, however, we must accept that it is out of our hands. Quebec doesn't own poutine. Variations of the dish have popped up elsewhere, and they will continue to do so. When a dish becomes globalized, it becomes something very different, something we need to accept.

PART IV

The Distinction

CHAPTER TEN

Is the Mighty Poutine …

Comfort Food?

The Guardian in the UK once called poutine "posh chips and gravy," the perfect hangover food.[1] Others have called poutine comfort food, or even an appetizer. Yet most would agree that poutine is just plain junk food that can be consumed at any time throughout the day. Poutine has gained its popularity by serving several dietary purposes, and its fame is likely related to the dish's versatility.[2] There is some evidence that our modern way of life is slowly destroying the three-meal institution as we know it. Most Canadians don't eat three times a day at specific hours, and out-of-household food consumption is at an all-time high. Snacks and grab-and-go solutions are very much part of many Canadians' lives today.

In my own life, no two days are the same. As it is for many people, my travel schedule, meetings, last-minute interviews, and other obligations often disrupt my plan to sit down and eat a proper meal. That's just the way it is. We conducted a study a few years ago at Dalhousie University that suggested that people eat alone most of the time.[3] Other influences also prevent us from having a lot of time to eat, such as time pressure, stress, and being alone. I see this occurring every day with my colleagues and students. Colleagues tend to eat at their desks, while students often eat in class or while walking through campus. So, we shouldn't be surprised to see how prevalent comfort food or fast food has become in our daily lives.

In a nutshell, comfort food serves as a source of nostalgia, typically high in calories and associated with memories of childhood. Some comfort foods are meals, some are simple snacks. According to a study by Wansink, Cheney, and Chan, men prefer warm, hearty, meal-sized comfort foods, such as steak, casseroles, and soup, while women tend to prefer comfort foods that are more snack related, like ice cream and chocolate.[4] Younger people also prefer snacks compared to consumers over fifty-five.[5] Mood associations with guilt also underscore how one chooses different meals and snacks, often in subtle but powerful ways. People may avoid indulgent foods like desserts or fast food when they feel guilty, opting instead for items perceived as healthier or more "virtuous," such as salads, smoothies, or low-calorie snacks. Conversely, feelings of guilt can sometimes trigger compensatory eating – choosing comfort foods to soothe emotional discomfort. These decisions are rarely based on nutritional value alone; they're shaped by internalized beliefs about morality, self-control, and what constitutes "good" or "bad" eating. As a result, the emotional weight of guilt can significantly influence not just what people eat, but how they perceive their own choices and behaviors around food.[6]

Stress can also be a factor in meal choice and push someone toward junk food or comfort food. Interestingly, studies show that men's comfort food consumption tends to be motivated by positive emotions, whereas women's consumption may be triggered by negative emotions.[7]

Certain comfort foods can enhance the relationships we have with one another, but lonely people also seek out comfort food as a means of coping.[8] In other words, a dish like poutine can unite us as much as it can be a painful reminder of our loneliness. Indeed, research on comfort food suggests that it can mean different things to different people depending on their state of mind. Our reactions to our surroundings may cause us to seek solace in comfort food, whether it's good for us or not.[9]

As Canadians, we live in a comparatively cold, harsh environment. Could poutine have been invented elsewhere? After all, poutine's basic ingredients are available in many other places around the world. In northern climates we often need comfort food to keep us warm, happy, and united. Poutine represents an escape, something that allows us to get our minds off our worries and everyday pressures. A poutine can be a parenthesis, a pause, that we all need from time to time.[10] The fact that the dish was invented in Canada, in Quebec, may not be a coincidence.

A National Brand?

A nation can be branded in many ways. Its reputation is shaped by a combination of media coverage, exports, cultural practices, and historical narratives. Certain countries become closely linked with specific elements of their identity – be it cuisine, architecture, public celebrations, or global enterprises. These associations form over time through repeated exposure and international engagement. When we think of different countries, particular images, sounds, or tastes often come to mind instantly, shaped by what those nations share with the world and how they are portrayed or perceived across borders.

When I travelled to China for the first time, I was excited to eat authentic Chinese food. To my surprise, authentic Chinese food is a lot different from what is served to us in Canada. Each Chinese province has its own dishes and traditions, unheard of in the West, made according to the ingredients available there. In North America, Chinese food is synonymous with sweet and sour chicken balls and chop suey. Chinese cuisine is much more sophisticated than that.[11] But unlike cuisines from other nations, Chinese food has not been truly globalized in its authentic form, in part because Chinese culture tends to be more inward-looking. While Chinese restaurants are widespread, the food served internationally is often a highly adapted version tailored to local tastes – far removed from the vast regional diversity found within China itself. Dishes like General Tso's chicken or fortune cookies, for instance, are virtually nonexistent in China. Of course, the same can be said about many other cuisines – Italian, Mexican, Indian – which have also undergone significant transformation to suit foreign palates. Yet with Chinese cuisine, the gap between perception and reality is especially pronounced.

By contrast, American culture – driven by a deep-seated belief in the universality of the American dream – has aggressively promoted its ideals and lifestyle abroad. Through powerful global brands and multinational corporations, some Americans genuinely believe they are spreading progress and even saving the world from itself. This missionary zeal stands in stark contrast to China's more contained cultural approach, which has resulted in a cuisine that, while omnipresent, is often misunderstood or misrepresented outside its homeland.[12]

Some nations have mastered specific meals. The English have greatly influenced how we see breakfast in North America: eggs, bacon, sausages, waffles, and hash browns. Breakfast is recognized as the most important meal of the day. This slogan was first introduced by cereal companies in North America in the early twentieth century. In China, the idea of particular breakfast foods is just not a concept people understand. There, breakfast consists of a mixture of vegetables, rice, meat and several types of breads.[13]

Americans have done an exemplary job exporting their foods. Very few countries do not have a McDonald's, Starbucks, or other well-known franchises. These have become symbols of an entire nation and its place in the world. Eric Schlosser's book, *Fast Food Nation*, covers some ground on this issue.[14] Schlosser argues that America branded itself as the dominant provider of junk food, food that is often intertwined with unhealthy lifestyles.

Other cuisines have survived and conquered the world with the help of emigration. Italy, France, India, Lebanon, Pakistan, and many other nations have exported their knowledge in the kitchen. Some cultures, such as the Greeks, have had success in restaurant management, no matter what cuisine they opt to serve to their clientele.[15] The world is travelling more, enhancing our collective curiosity for different types of food. Today, we celebrate all sorts of international cuisines.

But, of course, food trades go both ways. Take the example of rice. Rice is the main staple of every major Asian cuisine. In many Asian countries, particularly among the younger generations of affluent Asians, the rising popularity of Italian and Spanish cuisine, along with pastry, pizza, and other wheat-based food products, is causing many Asians to think differently about rice.[16]

Many nations have been successful in globalizing their culture, products, and cuisine. From a food perspective, I've always wondered what Canada's gift to the world is. Canola is certainly one obvious example. Canola is a genetically engineered form of rapeseed oil that was designed in Manitoba in 1978. Canola is known around the world, but it is also chastised as a genetically modified organism (GMO).[17] Years of poor risk communication around genetic engineering have left Canada in the middle of a highly polarized debate. Rather than engaging the public with transparency, nuance, and clear distinctions between different types of biotechnology, early efforts often dismissed public concerns or relied on overly technical explanations that failed to resonate. This breakdown in dialogue has created deep mistrust among segments of the population, fuelling fears and misconceptions about GMOs. As a result, canola – one of Canada's most significant agricultural innovations and a potential source of national pride – has also become a lightning rod for controversy. While many recognize its economic and agronomic value, others view it as emblematic of a food system shaped by secrecy and corporate interests. The failure to build a foundation of trust and scientific literacy around genetic engineering continues to cloud public perception and policy discussions to this day.[18]

Other obvious foods are maple syrup, Canadian peameal bacon, and mustard seeds. There are also fruits such as wild blueberries and saskatoon berries. These commodities are known to the world. According to *Reader's Digest*,[19] the top Canadian dishes are ketchup flavoured snacks, tourtière, split pea soup, Nanaimo bars, butter tarts, "Canadian" pizza, BeaverTails, the Caesar cocktail, and Canadian peameal bacon. The number one Canadian dish on the list is poutine, which is described as "perhaps one of the country's most outlandish and defining dishes." Putting aside the drink (the Caesar), the condiment (ketchup), and the meat (Canadian bacon), the unhealthiness and simplicity of these dishes is quite striking. However, most of these dishes aren't known to the world, with the exception of poutine.

All this is evidence that poutine is part of our national identity. How large a part, and whether it has the potential to redefine the way others see us and how we see ourselves, is a fundamental question.

An Event Magnet?

Social events that celebrate food are not a new concept. We see them everywhere celebrating dishes, a specific region, or even a commodity, bringing people together and reminding them how important food is in our lives. Many villages in rural Quebec have festivals of their own. Some of the ones I attended while growing up were quite strange. Sorel has its gibelotte (rabbit stew) festival, Gib Fest. Few know what gibelotte is, but over fifty thousand people have been going to the event each year since 1977.[20] In Asbestos (yes, there is a city named after asbestos), I once participated in a parade called the "Festival des Gourmands" in 1989. The city ran this event every year to bring people to the city and think of something other than the cancer-causing asbestos, I suppose. I had fun riding a float and giving away pieces of meat that we were barbequing. The event was all about food, any food for anyone to enjoy and celebrate without prejudice.

Bringing people together to celebrate food is always fun. Today, poutine seems to be an excuse for many communities to get together, everywhere around the world, as it is seen as a powerful, festive combination between fun, indulgence, and pleasure. The number of local events centred around poutine is exploding. Most events that are related to poutine did not begin until the mid-2000s, but since 2012 there has been a significant expansion, not just in Canada, but also in New Hampshire, Vermont, and other smaller states. A global event to celebrate poutine does not exist, at least not yet. But there is an increasing number of events outside Quebec, where poutine was not all that well-known just a few years go.

Most cities in Canada now have events that at least feature poutine. One of the most well-known takes place each August in Drummondville and is called "le Festival de la Poutine." It is a three-day event, filled with shows, chefs, activities for children, and more. The event started in 2008 and now attracts people from all over Quebec. An average year will attract roughly twenty-five thousand people, and the event sells more than ten thousand poutines. The idea was initially launched as a joke, a gesture by the members of the Quebec rock band called Les Trois Accords to claim, in the name of Drummondville, the origin of poutine. It would not be surprising to see this event expand even more in years to come.

Montreal also has events to celebrate poutine. Grand Poutinefest is a gathering of the best street food trucks in Quebec. Each food truck offers more original and delicious versions of the dish. Live music, children's games, fairground games – it's a real intergenerational picnic that moves from city to city. The proceeds from the events go to local causes centred on youth and sport. The Grand Poutinefest not only happens in the Old Port of Montreal, but it also travels all over the province. It is a road show of sorts, or a circus for poutine. Grand Poutinefest is not as popular as the one in Drummondville, but it draws a lot of tourists and gets them to try poutine, possibly for the very first time.

Toronto has several events to celebrate poutine. The most well-known is Poutine, at Yonge and Dundas. They bring restaurants together to serve the best poutine in town. That event runs in May. In October, at the same location, the World Eating Poutine Championships are held. It started in 2010 and is sponsored by Smoke's Poutinerie. The event also raises funds for charity.

Every year, in early February, restaurants from different cities across Canada make special poutines just for La Poutine Week. The event began in Montreal in 2012 and has since received a lot of attention. It has hundreds of thousands of participating establishments. Unlike poutine events that are organized in the summer, Poutine Week takes place in the middle of winter. Throughout that week, restaurants across Canada and the United States make special poutines to participate. Poutine lovers across the nation get a chance to enjoy new tasty poutines and vote for their favourite ones.

The Ultimate Shareable Dish?

Poutine is an unusual dish in many ways. It is designed to be consumed minutes after being served. There is no such thing as leftover poutine. Once a poutine is served, there is limited time to eat it before it becomes unappetizing. Poutine also can be shared and eaten by more than one person. You regularly see a portion of poutine being served with two or three forks. In my conversations with restaurateurs, this fact was noted several times. Unlike other iconic dishes or fast-food items, how poutine has been socialized has defined the dish over the years. You can argue that pizza is often eaten by more than one person, but a pizza is divided into individual slices. When a group eats poutine, they share the portion from the same container.

We all eat out of necessity, but in some countries the social component of dining is much more prominent. Sharing a meal represents an opportunity to get to know other people. In some places, meal preparation is a form of art, something to be appreciated and commented upon as a group.[21]

In North America, the collective experience of sharing food seems to be of less importance. Dishes are often individualized and served for one person, proportioned properly for any given diet. Servings are meant to be customized.[22] Food sharing is a daily reality for many people around the world, especially in China. Eating and sharing meals with family members, friends, and even community members is a common practice in both daily life and social events.[23]

Food is a vital element for society and plays an important role not only as a source of nutrition but also in one's daily life. Food cultivation, harvesting, serving, and eating habits are culturally defined and make up a central element to our social lives as human beings, helping us develop interpersonal relationships in our socio-cultural environments. Various messages can be transmitted through different kinds of foods, indicating the relationship proximity among people. No matter how a meal is prepared, the realness of that connection cannot be replaced.

Eating and sharing meals is a basic element of society, and no culture has been established without food sharing.[24] In addition to the social aspect of sharing meals, it is a way for a culture to let peers know which food is edible. Sharing a meal can foster a sense of equality and mutual understanding among participants. Around the table, social hierarchies often dissolve, at least temporarily – nobody is inherently above anyone else, and everyone is given a place and a voice. This inclusivity can make all members of a group feel welcome, seen, and valued. The act of eating together humanizes participants, reinforcing empathy and connection across lines of class, age, or background. The goal of socializing a meal is, at its core, to make the experience more democratic.

That said, this is not always the case. Power dynamics, cultural expectations, or even seating arrangements can reintroduce hierarchy and exclusion into the shared meal. In some contexts, meals can reinforce social divisions – who eats first, who is served, and what is served can all reflect underlying inequalities. So while shared meals often *aspire* to level the playing field, they can also mirror the broader structures and tensions within a society.

Biological and geographical conditions, as well as cultural norms, define the eating behaviours within a family or group by shaping what foods are available, acceptable, and desirable. Biologically, dietary needs may differ based on age, health, or metabolism, influencing meal composition and frequency. Geographical factors – such as climate, soil quality, and proximity to water – determine which crops and animals can be raised or foraged, directly impacting a community's staple foods. Meanwhile, cultural norms dictate how food is prepared, when meals are eaten, and who participates. These norms often reflect deep-rooted beliefs, religious practices, traditions, and social hierarchies. Together, these factors form a complex ecosystem that influences not only what is consumed, but how food is shared, valued, and passed down through generations.[25]

Serving food also comes with obligations and responsibilities that go beyond the simple act of nourishment. In many cultures, the person who prepares or serves a meal holds an important social role, often associated with care, respect, and even authority. Sharing a meal creates a collective experience, and with it comes the expectation that responsibilities – such as cooking, setting the table, serving, cleaning up, or offering thanks – will be distributed among participants. This division of labour not only eases the workload but reinforces a sense of community, mutual support, and accountability. It reflects an unspoken agreement: everyone contributes to the well-being of the group, either directly through action or indirectly through appreciation and participation. In this way, the act of serving and sharing food becomes a reflection of the values and structure of the group itself.

Therefore, food leads to mutual obligations among relatives and the community. The social connection that meal sharing brings is also about who is in and who is not. Relationships are usually started by an offer of food sharing. A refusal of meal sharing results in the rejection of a social connection.[26] When considering food as a social catalyst, its power goes way beyond just consuming it. Food preparation is relevant to the level of power of the sharer and is also associated with the conflicts between social classes, ethnic groups, and nations. Certain types of food define social classes and groups, excluding certain individuals. Meal sharing cuts through all of that, and, as I see it, a dish like poutine fits squarely in the category of shareable foods. Poutine is affordable, simple, and doesn't discriminate against anyone. Beef and lobster, among many other dishes, are not as conveniently accessible from a social or financial perspective. So, in a way, it is completely normal to see poutine being shared by so many in a social setting. It is almost as if the dish were designed for that.

Whether it is to catch up with friends, to negotiate an important deal, or share values among individuals, eating together has always been a part in the processes of promoting and safeguarding peace between people, families, and friends. Many people live in isolation and need to break free from their shell. Connecting while eating is an easy therapy for many, so perhaps poutine would be suitable for some of these special settings.[27]

Sharing a poutine brings people together and creates a different experience for each person. One bite may be mostly cheese with fries and some gravy, while the next bite may only have fries, or, depending on the variety of poutine, a completely different ingredient, such as sausage or green peppers. People share their experiences while eating the poutine, bite after every bite.

A Side Dish or a Meal?

Poutine is served in many ways. Most of the time, I've had it as a meal. But many chains and restaurants offer poutine as a side dish, which always strikes me as peculiar. Given the popularity of poutine, restaurant menus now offer customers the option to replace fries with poutine. It seems like a lot of food for a side dish, but if you are unfamiliar with poutine, this could be an easy way to try it. Side dishes are meant to be complementary, yet poutine adds considerable caloric weight to a meal. Poutine is also considered as an appetizer by some cultures as well. Lunch, dinner, or snack – it can be confusing at times where the dish fits.[28] To understand how poutine fits in our daily lives, I want to take a step back and examine our daily eating habits.

The way meals are structured in Canada has been redefined over time. Canada's culinary traditions have been influenced by other countries for the most part. In Quebec, France has influenced how people eat in the province the most. Chefs and cooking shows often refer to France to justify particular choices and trend-setting picks. France's history in the kitchen is so rich, so powerful, it is hardly ever ignored. Traditions around cheeses and bakery products make it obvious.[29] The cultural definition of an appropriate meal is a major determinant of meal size and composition, influencing how a dish is perceived and how it would fit in a person's daily routine of three meals. A successful dish needs to align with this well-known meal pattern, and poutine is indeed now served in many different forms to be appropriate for breakfast, lunch, or dinner.

Dinner is usually composed of three main parts: a starter, a main dish, and dessert. Cheese can also be added somewhere to complement these three components. In everyday life, consumers often choose to eat either a starter with a main dish, or a main dish with a dessert. Interestingly, the choice of an appetizer or starter influences decisions about the rest of the meal. For example, if the appetizer is high in calories or fat, consumers tend to choose something different for their main course, something lighter and healthier.[30] This is how most Canadians are raised and what they are accustomed to.

In a restaurant, starters and main dishes are often consumed. A meal is not complete unless both elements are included. A drink can also be involved. Of course, the content of the main dish may vary according to the gender, age, and level of education of the consumer. Women tend to eat more white meats and vegetables, while men tend to eat more beef. Consumers in Canada and other places also follow culinary scripts, known as implicit rules, to construct their meals, considering the type of food, and the context: place, time, and company.[31] In addition, a close association has been found between the eating occasion (lunch, dinner, snacking, etc.), the eating location (at home, at work, on a camping trip, in transit, etc.), and the foods chosen when constructing a meal.[32]

These are large influencing factors when constructing a meal for oneself and are seen throughout the industrialized world.[33] In a very unspoken way, whatever the type of meal, some elements tend to play a central role in the composition of the main dish. Proteins and starches are prevalent elements in most people's diets and influence how we consume food. Poutine has both.

Most consumers construct their meal around their choice of meat, or a source of protein. Vegetables and starches are added after. In the case of fast food, the focus is often very similar. The one frequent exception is pizza, which again makes it such an appropriate comparator to poutine. Both can be served without meat but include cheese, which is the main source of protein. Starch is also key to both dishes.[34] The traditional focus on certain elements of a meal could be a barrier to promoting a different dish in favour of satisfying several different demographics. Gender, education, and nutritional awareness are also key determinants when picking new combinations. Poutine offers a unique but simple solution and a model that, like pizza, is endlessly adaptable.[35] Anything can be added to it to accommodate any taste or occasion.[36]

The versatility of the dish itself has allowed poutine to occupy many different roles. It goes beyond the three main meals, or any parts of a standard meal for that matter. It is mostly used as a main dish, to be shared among friends or family. Poutine can also be a side dish, which allows people to discover the dish, beyond fries, mashed potatoes, or any other classics we know.

A Pricey Dish?

Price is always an important factor when choosing what to eat. Some options – organic, gluten-free, locally grown, etc. – dramatically increase the cost of eating. Consumers with less means are more affected than others, often leaving fast food as their only option.[37] Expensive convenience foods are also a consideration because of our limited time for cooking and busy lifestyles.[38]

The connection between food prices and food choices has been studied over the years. Much of the published research addresses the relationship between food prices and production, expenditure, and consumption.[39] Of particular relevance is the connection between food prices and dietary intake across income levels as individuals of low income are typically more sensitive to changes in food prices.[40] Unsurprisingly, consumers with lower incomes will tend to have less varied, lower quality diets compared to consumers with higher incomes.[41] Consumers feel more food secure if they believe that they can afford to feed themselves.[42]

For some individuals and groups, fast food can give a sense of food security.[43] Affordability is rarely a concern for consumers shopping for fast food, even though the price of one meal can be expensive.[44] The price of poutine has never been an issue for most people. Consumers want to try the dish, eat it as a treat, or have a snack to complete an evening out with friends and family. Poutine is not a luxury, but if eaten too often, it may be taxing for one's body. Affordability, or a lack thereof, has not affected poutine's reputation.

Poutine prices tend to vary between $3 and almost $20, depending on the ingredients. The original poutine sold in Warwick was $0.35 in 1957. In today's money, that is a little less than $4, so most poutines are more expensive today than when first created. When I was living in Farnham, a regular-sized poutine cost $2.50, and it was enough to fill the stomach of a growing boy. Today, the same poutine is $7.20, which is the same as the price in Toronto.

Typically, the average price is around $10. At times, poutine is offered as a side dish, which sells for $2 to $4 extra. The labour required to make a poutine can be significant, mainly in making fries. Peeling, cutting, and frying all take time. Most places will opt for frozen fries, but many upscale places use fresh potatoes. Chez Ashton only uses fresh potatoes, which is why prices are higher than average. Cheese curds can cost anywhere between $2.50 to $3 for one hundred grams. The amount of cheese in the poutine also varies from one restaurant to another, and one recipe to another. Some restaurants add cheese on the top and bottom of the poutine, which also increases the overall price. The gravy can be made days in advance, and the quality varies from one outlet to another as well.

When I toured the world looking for poutine, I ended up paying anywhere between CAD$12 to $15 for a serving of poutine. The quality was spotty, but my expectations were not unrealistic considering my location. Expecting an original poutine overseas was perhaps wishful thinking, but prices were generally much higher than the prices you find in Quebec.

Some have attempted to build the most expensive poutine possible. In 2018, Smoke's Poutinerie created the most expensive poutine in Canada at the premiere of *Crazy Rich Asians*. Pairing the expensive poutine with this film was appropriate, as the story is about a Chinese American professor who travels to Singapore with her boyfriend only to discover that he is from a very wealthy family. The event took place during the Toronto International Film Festival (TIFF), so there were thousands of visitors from all over the world in Toronto at that time. Pairing the event with the most expensive poutine gave the dish global attention among affluent socialites. The poutine was made with ingredients that are familiar to many: a whole lobster, wagyu steak, truffle oil, caviar, shiitake and chanterelle mushrooms, kimchi, and edible orchids. The entire ensemble of unusual ingredients was covered with $100 worth of gold flakes. The price? $448.17 for one poutine.[45]

In addition to price, size is something enterprising restaurant owners and chefs have experimented with as well. Many large poutines have been made to break the record of the largest poutine ever, but the one by Smoke's Poutinerie is the most expensive that I know of. When you think about it, building an expensive poutine is counterintuitive, given that poutine should be an affordable mixture of inexpensive ingredients. This isn't surprising, though, given that poutine is changing. People often believe that these foods, like other fast foods, are beneath them. Offering an expensive poutine puts the humble dish in a different light, at an event where many people value money, fame, and materialism. If poutine is for all people, and that includes the wealthy, who may be interested in something new or strange.[46]

If poutine was something one could make more easily at home, things might be somewhat different. I remember trying to make poutine at home and failing miserably. My cooking skills aren't the best, but given the simplicity of the dish, I thought I could make it happen. It really boiled down to texture and taste. My sister-in-law, who is on a keto diet, prepared her own version of a poutine at home. It was an interesting take on the humble dish, but it was not the same as ordering one at the restaurant. Not even close.

PART V

The Pilgrimage

CHAPTER ELEVEN

Following the Poutine: A Pilgrimage

Visiting the Location(s) Where It Started

In researching this book, I decided to visit the places that define poutine's history. I also wanted to meet and talk with key people who helped create poutine and have witnessed its rise in popularity. Some of the locations that take credit for the creation of poutine include the Acadie, Matane, Plessisville, Princeville, Victoriaville and Saguenay. However, there are only two locations that have actual artifacts, credible testimonials, and hard evidence to back up their claims: Drummondville and Warwick. These two places, therefore, are where I kicked off my poutine pilgrimage.

When visiting Warwick and Drummondville, you almost feel that both locations want the debate about poutine's origins to continue. What's important for both locations is to see people talking about poutine. My sense is that neither town really sees the controversy as necessary to increase the popularity of poutine. As we all know by now, poutine is an iconic Canadian dish. When I spoke to people in these two locations about my travels and what has happened to the humble dish over the last forty years, they were both shocked and amazed.

The challenge with Warwick is that the original restaurant no longer exists and finding anyone to interview is difficult. Both Mr. and Mrs. Lachance have since passed away. I did manage to get in touch with Warwick's historical society and was able to connect with key individuals from the town that way. Warwick is similar to my own hometown, so I was looking forward to the visit. I also had to pay a visit to two individuals who helped to make poutine famous: Ashton Leblond, the founder of Chez Ashton, and Ryan Smolkin, the founder of Smoke's Poutinerie.

Drummondville and Warwick: Poutine's Ground Zero

While nobody will ever know for certain who created poutine, Drummondville and Warwick both have strong claims to the title and my visits to both these towns were informative.

The small town of Warwick, known for its cheese, lies in the Bois-Francs Region, Arthabaska County, about fifty kilometres from Trois-Rivières and just a few kilometres from Victoriaville. Many in Warwick claim that Fernand Lachance invented poutine in 1957. The town itself

Photo 11.1. My visit to Warwick, Quebec.

reminded me of my hometown of Farnham. It is about one hundred kilometres from my hometown yet I had never visited Warwick before. The town was founded in 1861, and the population is just shy of five thousand people. Warwick consists of a couple of main streets and a few stores here and there. As you arrive in the town, a Tim Hortons greets you. Right across the street is a small restaurant called Victoria, which makes cheese curds. Up until the 1980s, textile manufacturing was a significant economic sector in Warwick. During World War II, the textile sector was a significant contributor everywhere in rural Quebec, but it has since collapsed, forcing towns to either diversify or face decline and eventual disappearance. In Warwick's case, the focus became dairy and cheese. In fact, in 2007 Warwick was officially registered in the province as "Quebec's capital of fine cheese."

Photo 11.2. Location where the father of the original poutine, Fernand Lachance, operated his restaurant in 1957.

Within seconds of driving into town, you come to Warwick's city hall, which was built in 1860, the year before the town's foundation. It is a beautiful building, typical of a town like this. My hometown of Farnham also has a nice city hall, prominently located near the river. The river in Warwick is not as centrally located, skirting the southwest edge of town. I was headed to Warwick's "Maison de la Culture," the old train station converted to exhibit artifacts from the town's history. The building is charming and has become a shrine for people who want to know more about Warwick's history.

As I entered the old train station, I was immediately greeted by André Moreau and Guy Raîche. Guy works for the town and is responsible for its archives and history. André is a volunteer, a retired executive director of the local school board. We chatted for about an hour about my research and what I had discovered about Warwick. There was an exhibit in the building about cheese and the story of poutine, along with many artifacts.

The exhibit was set up for an event that they were organizing – an attempt to set a record for the world's largest poutine! They were selling tickets for ten dollars each. More than six thousand people attended the event, and they did manage to set a new world record. I had no idea it was going on until they told me. Poutine was clearly a source of pride to the people of Warwick, and they undoubtedly felt the need to position the town as the birthplace of poutine. Both Guy and André were incredibly hospitable and generous with their time and showed me around the exhibit. There was a lot of information about cheesemaking and many articles about the famed Fernand Lachance, the father of the original poutine, as I understand it.

The Father of Poutine

Fernand Lachance was born on August 27, 1917, and died on February 6, 2004, which is right about the time poutine was becoming well-known around the world. "Mr. Poutine" as he was known, had six children with his wife, Germaine Lettre Lachance, and the family lived a few doors away from their restaurant, Café Idéal. A few years later, the restaurant became Le Lutin Qui Rit. In 1957, Jean-Guy Lainesse made history by asking Lachance to mix cheese and fries together rather than serve them separately. Twenty-five years old at the time, Lainesse was a trucker, doing deliveries between small cities and stopping at regular spots. He was the first person to ask Fernand Lachance to mix fries and cheese together.[1] In that same year, the gravy-free poutine was added to the

Photo 11.3. Copy of the first known menu with the word "poutine," used in 1957.

menu, making Lachance the first ever to add the word "poutine" to its menu. The authentic version of the poutine was born. A copy of the menu is in Warwick's Maison de la Culture and can be seen by anyone who travels there.

Lachance believed that a true poutine should not include gravy. His wife Germaine, however, was a talented cook and thought a gravy would complement the mixture. The sauce she prepared was ketchup-based and sold as a side dish in 1962. In light of this, I would argue Germaine should be credited for her contribution to the invention, making Fernand and Germaine together the "father and mother" of the original poutine. History was made in Warwick before anything happened in Drummondville.

Unfortunately, Lutin Qui Rit no longer operates, and a beauty salon now stands at the location. There is no plaque on the site or anything commemorating it. That's what's missing in Warwick. Drummondville, on the other hand, is a much

Photo 11.4. Le Roy Jucep, in Drummondville, Quebec, where the modern poutine as we know it today was invented.

larger town, and the original restaurant that served poutine remains. They have pictures, an operating location, and evidence. Other than the menu and anecdotal stories, Warwick doesn't have much to show. When you visit Warwick, though, you can tell something special happened there in 1957.

In Drummondville, Jean-Paul Roy gave the world the modern poutine as we know it today. While the Lachances gave the world the first taste of what was to come, Roy was the true inventor of the modern poutine.

Drummondville and Le Roy Jucep

In Drummondville, I visited Le Roy Jucep. Drummondville is a city of one hundred thousand people, just forty-five minutes away from my hometown. Midway between

Montreal and Quebec City, Drummondville is a common waypoint between the two larger cities. I knew little about Drummondville beyond the restaurants and gas stations you see when driving along the main strip. Drummondville has changed over the years. Like in most cities, the youth leave town to attend university, and they rarely come back. Many companies are in the service industry now, which doesn't provide the quality jobs people are looking for.

Le Roy Jucep was easy to find on the main street, where it has been since 1964. It's a surprisingly unpretentious, cozy little place with parking spaces on both sides, similar to the kind at drive-in restaurants that were popular in the 1960s and '70s. There's a patio in front of the restaurant and, all in all, it is a normal-looking diner. Unless you were aware of the history of Le Roy Jucep, you would never be able to tell the place is famous for serving the first modern poutine.

Initially, Le Roy Jucep was just a little shack of about 150 square feet. As time passed and customer expectations evolved, it developed into a decent-looking restaurant. The shack moved once, in the '60s, to what is now called St-Joseph Boulevard in Drummondville. In the 1960s, the boulevard was not what it is today. It was more modest and less busy. Today, St-Joseph Boulevard connects to the TransCanada highway and has been developed much more extensively as a result of that connection.

I arrived at 11 a.m. and found a few people already there, perhaps ten people in all. Staff outnumbered the number of patrons, but I could tell they were preparing for the rush hour. There is a unique feel when you enter the restaurant. It's like nothing has changed in fifty years, but it doesn't feel tired or

Photo 11.5. Mylène Héroux, general manager of Le Roy Jucep.

rundown. Most of the employees are older women, but there are some younger women working there as well. The patrons were mostly older as well, the kind of regular customers that keep restaurants like this one in business through the years. The colour scheme was white, orange, and brown – not fashionable colours. The restaurant was bright but not too bright. You could sit at the counter and eat on your own while chatting with the servers or eat in the dining room.

Another striking feature of the restaurant was the number of celebrity pictures on its walls, some dating back fifty years. Many politicians have been there, including prime ministers, most likely during a campaign. Most of the pictures I recognized; many of the people in them have since passed away. I felt like I was the only person looking at the pictures as I'm sure the regulars have seen them countless times. I also noticed pieces of a sugar pie behind the front counter. Just a typical diner you would find in any city in the '50s and '60s. At Roy Jucep, time stands still, yet the atmosphere is far from stale. A certificate of authenticity hangs on the wall, which shows that Le Roy Jucep was where the modern poutine was created.

Photo 11.6. Inside Le Roy Jucep in Drummondville, Quebec.

The restaurant is now owned by a couple of local investors. Le Roy Jucep employs almost fifty people and sells over seventy-two thousand poutines per year. That's almost two hundred poutines a day. The most popular poutine is the "authentique," followed by the "poutine du Roy" mixed with hot dogs. They also offer a poutine of the month. The restaurant sources its ingredients from local farmers and processors. Some of the processing is done outside the restaurant, but a lot of it is done internally.

I met with the general manager, Mylène Héroux. She came out to greet me, exuding efficiency, leadership skills, and an approachable attitude, exactly the attributes you want in a general manager. We sat at a table in the dining area where Mylène explained that she regularly does interviews with reporters and students. This was the first time she had met with a researcher.

Photo 11.7. Famous celebrities and politicians at Le Roy Jucep over the years.

Our conversation was very casual. Mylène is originally from Drummondville and has spent most her life there. She has some training in operations management, but not in hospitality per se. She went to Montreal for her studies but came back to Drummondville to be close to her family. Mylène has spent her career in the food service industry, which can be tough, with long hours working nights, weekends, and holidays. She's been in the business for more than twenty years and was working at another establishment when an investor called to ask her to take over Le Roy Jucep. At the time, Mylène did not realize what it meant to run Le Roy Jucep. She saw it as a regular position at a normal restaurant. She now recognizes that Le Roy Jucep is different and that managing the restaurant entails more than it does at other places.

Mylène truly enjoys the diverse nature of the job. You never know what will happen in a restaurant, and Mylène admits that, two years in, she is still learning and adapting.

The owners help her deal with managerial issues, as they also manage other businesses.

Mylène never met Mr. Roy, or at least, she doesn't recall meeting him. She mentioned that Mr. Roy was a trained saucier, which may explain why the sauce is so critical to his poutine. Before 1964, cheese was always served as a side dish. Mr. Roy, she claims, mixed these ingredients to make the poutine as we know it. Mylène believes that the cook, Ti-Pout, mixed together the ingredients, and the dish was named after him as a result.

Mylène believes that what makes Le Roy Jucep's poutine special is the sauce. Anyone can make fries and cheese curds, but the sauce makes it a unique experience. She noted that people make special orders and ask to have the cheese under the fries, not over. Traditionally, curds are served on top at Le Roy Jucep. For her, poutine is part of Quebec's cultural fabric, and most Quebecers need to eat a poutine at some point. She added that poutine is emotional for Quebecers. One of the best comfort foods, it is Quebec's gift to the world.

Mylène was proud to say that she went out with her father to eat poutine at Le Roy Jucep. It was a special moment for her, a way to connect with her father. She also observed that so many of the customers are getting older. Some have been visiting every day for decades. Mylène also mentioned that the demand is affected by what's on television. Fewer people show up to buy a poutine if a popular show is on. Previously open twenty-four hours a day, the restaurant's hours have recently changed, and it is now open until 1 a.m.

What's shocking, after all these years, is that Le Roy Jucep has only one location. As Mylène explained to me, labour

Photo 11.8. Lunch at Le Roy Jucep with my family.

issues are a major obstacle to expansion. It is too difficult to hire people to support another restaurant. We also talked about how poutine has become a global phenomenon. This still surprises Mylène and people local to the area for whom poutine is, first and foremost, a dish from Quebec, a dish that represents Quebec's identity.

After chatting for a while, we ordered a poutine. How could I possibly visit poutine's birthplace without trying it? I was intrigued by the menu. A total of twenty-four different poutines were available. Mylène suggested I try the traditional, and she ordered the poutine of the month, a Mexican version with peppers, beef, and olives. As we waited, we continued to discuss management and how challenging it is to manage a restaurant today.

When the poutine arrived, it was huge. The smell reminded me of my childhood. As I tasted my first bite, I realized how different this poutine was. Just as Mylène had said, the sauce made all the difference. Mr. Roy's legacy. The sauce meshed everything together, the cheese curds, the fries, everything. It was simple but amazingly good. My initial plan was to eat a small portion, just to get an idea of what Le Roy Jucep was about. I ended up eating the entire portion. I also tried the poutine of the month, which was quite tasty. While not exactly to my taste – I much prefer the original version – I can see how people may get curious to try something else. After being away from Quebec for so long, I just wanted the traditional poutine.

I left Drummondville feeling like I'd relived part of my childhood. Something felt right. The spirit of Roy Jucep is alive and well there. It is represented by some employees who have worked there for well over fifty years, such as Yolande. Yolande started working there at fourteen in 1965. She lived near the restaurant, right next to it, in fact. I was amazed when she told me this. People working during the day shift have worked for Le Roy Jucep for over twenty years. Some people in the kitchen have worked there for thirty-five years. Pride runs deep in this restaurant, and the employees are fully committed to it.

What happened at Le Roy Jucep many years ago made history, and I was happy to have met the caretakers of Mr. Roy's legacy. There are establishments much like Le Roy Jucep in small towns throughout rural Quebec, but it is unique, an example of pure entrepreneurship that has left a lasting mark. As I pulled out of Le Roy Jucep's parking lot, I promised myself that I would bring my children there one day. I owed it to them. They needed to know what poutine tastes like, or what it should taste like.

Ambassador: Meeting the Godfather of Poutine

In Warwick and Drummondville, I gained an intimate sense of where poutine came from and who was responsible for

Photo 11.9. With the godfather of modern poutine, Ashton Leblond.

its creation. But neither Lachance nor Roy made poutine famous. One individual really believed in poutine and made the dish a staple item for his business – Ashton Leblond.

Ashton Leblond's[2] story is about passion and authenticity. Leblond is president and owner of the restaurant chain Chez Ashton, which is known today for its poutine. There are twenty-five Chez Ashton locations in the Quebec City region. Many credit Leblond as the inventor of poutine, but he is not. While poutine was created by a series of fortunate coincidences, Leblond's belief in poutine as a product was anything but an accident. The more I read and learned about him, the more I wanted to meet the man. I was finally able to sit down with him in one of his restaurants in downtown Quebec City.

After a bit of a mix-up, I found Mr. Leblond waiting for me at the Boulevard Charest location, right downtown Quebec City, known as the St-Roch district. It was 11 a.m., so the restaurant was not too busy. He greeted me warmly enough, but I sensed a bit of skepticism about the purpose of our interview and why in the world I wanted to write a book about poutine. I stressed right away that the book was not about him and that I only hoped to get his view on poutine. He appeared to relax, and our conversation started.[3]

Leblond is very soft-spoken and unassuming. For someone who has achieved so much, this was unexpected. He seemed accessible, and I felt that I could ask any question I wanted. I was drawn to Ashton Leblond because of his story. I learned that we both came from the Eastern Townships and that we were both influenced by farming in our youths. But our similarities ended there.

To recap, Leblond was born on March 7, 1948, in Saint-François-Xavier-de-Brampton, a small municipality located between Sherbrooke and Windsor in the Eastern Townships. This village is literally thirty minutes from my hometown. Leblond's childhood was anything but easy. He came from a family of seventeen children, two of whom died in early childhood.[4] He was the family's seventh child and was named after a lawyer who had inspired his parents. Like any kid working on a farm, he learned the meaning of effort, perseverance, and autonomy early on.[5] As he grew out of childhood, he couldn't see himself working as farmer or staying in the region. His ambition caused him to leave Saint-François-Xavier-de-Brampton at the young age of fourteen in 1962.

In 1965, at the age of seventeen, he ended up in Quebec City, where he worked for Champigny College as a cook, helper, and cleaner. He lived in a room just upstairs from where he worked. To make ends meet, he started to cook and sold meat pies door to door. For the next few years, Leblond worked hard and gained critical insights about business and people. While in Quebec City he met Augustin

Lord, who became his mentor and second father. To this day, Leblond is thankful for Augustin Lord's help and advice. In fact, in 2015 when he opened a new reception hall, Leblond named it after Lord.

Leblond had always been fascinated by "potato chip" wagons during his youth and had dreamed of doing something similar one day. In 1969, the opportunity Leblond had been waiting for happened. He saw that a "potato chip" wagon was for sale in the Sherbrooke region near the St-François River, close to the train station in the city. The "potato chip" wagon that was for sale was called Chez Laurette. Laurette wanted to sell and move on. Leblond bought it and kept the name until he replaced it with Ashton Snack-Bar, then Ashton Casse-Croûte to give it a French name. Leblond managed to purchase the wagon with his $700 in savings, some help from his father, and a loan. He was barely twenty-one years old and a full-time restaurateur. In 1969, the first Chez Ashton was born. At first, he ran the chip wagon from March to October, spending the winter months in Florida. This became impossible, though, as it was difficult to retain staff from one season to another. In 1977 the business became a year-round endeavour and expanded accordingly.

Leblond built his first restaurant across the street from where his chip wagon was located and opened his second restaurant in 1981, in Beauport. Soon after, he opened several more restaurants across the region, a total of twenty-five. Today, Chez Ashton sells more than four million pounds of potatoes and more than 617,000 pounds of cheese curds each year.

Coming from the Eastern Townships, Leblond was inspired to sell poutine in Quebec City. It took a while for poutine to take off, but he never gave up. He originally used a hot chicken sauce to bring the fries and curds together, but he had to make adjustments to his sauce before he got it perfect. What was difficult to sell was the cheese. Quebec City was not accustomed to eating cheese curds made from cheddar. As he told me: "I came from the Eastern Townships, and that's why I knew cheddar. But I quickly realized people in Quebec did not know cheddar at all. That is when I saw an opportunity." For years, he gave samples away for people to try the cheese curds. As Leblond noted, "The cheese is a key ingredient for a great poutine. It has to be fresh, and you can't use anything else but curds." Leblond believed in the dish when nobody else did. He prevailed and continued to sell it when others were telling him to stop. After years of perseverance, sales began to pick up soon after the opening of his second restaurant. Today, poutine represents almost 50 per cent of his sales.

Leblond is tight-lipped about how his sauce is made. Like Roy in Drummondville, Leblond believes the sauce is a critical element to poutine. He believes in freshness and purchases all of his products locally. His potatoes all come from l'Île d'Orléans nearby. Leblond clearly believes in serving his customers fresh, not frozen, foods. He has worked on a harvesting cycle for potatoes over several months in order to ensure the quality remains the same throughout the winter months.[6]

At the end of the interview, Leblond offered me a poutine, prepared and served by him. I asked for a Dulton poutine, one of his favourite dishes. It comes with fries, gravy, and cheese curds on top, along with ground beef and sausage.

It has all the right elements. It was exquisite. Eating a poutine that is served and prepared by the godfather of poutine himself was a special treat.

When I told Leblond that I considered him the godfather of poutine, he was surprised. I could tell that he did not realize how significant his contribution was or how popular poutine had become since he started his business. I told Leblond about my experiences around the world, and the rise of Smoke's Poutinerie. We also talked about the future of poutine, and he shared his concerns about food trends and the focus on unhealthy foods. But Leblond believes that poutine is not going away, and people will always need to feel human and indulge in some way. He told me that he was proud to offer his customers an escape, something they can enjoy, if only for a while.

I left with the impression that Leblond did not have an easy life. Some of his life challenges are well documented in a book called *Ashton Leblond: Juste du Vrai.*[7] This book is very personal, and it goes deep into the experiences that affected his personal life. I don't think he fully appreciated how much I respected his work and what he did for my culture, Quebec's culture, around the world. It was a privilege to meet him, and I felt it would have been nice to have met him years ago. I felt I could have learned much more from him.

Ashton Leblond was in the twilight of his career and thinking of selling his business. I could tell it was not going to be easy for him to emotionally let go of what he had built over the last fifty years. In 2017, reports suggested that the group MTY from Toronto offered Ashton Leblond $55 million for his chain of restaurants, with over 650 employees.

But he did end up selling. Chez Ashton was sold in early 2022. The acquisition was finalized on February 28, 2022, when the company was purchased by 9450-4214 Québec Inc., a firm owned by two young entrepreneurs from Saint-Raymond: Émily Adam and Jean-Christophe Lirette. The new owners, who also operate the Ti-Oui snack bar and several Harvey's franchises, aimed to preserve the chain's local roots while modernizing its brand. In November 2023, they rebranded Chez Ashton to simply "Ashton," unveiling a refreshed visual identity and initiating expansion plans beyond the Quebec City region.[8] As of 2025, Ashton operates twenty-five locations across Quebec, with continued ambitions for growth.

Five decades of fries and poutine, of selling a product he believed in. It is quite an incredible legacy.[9] Tourists now consider Ashton an important place to stop and enjoy poutine.[10] I have met a lot of inspiring entrepreneurs in the food industry, but Ashton Leblond is different. His business moto has always been "juste du frais, juste du vrai!" ("just fresh, just real"). And that's exactly what he is.

CHAPTER TWELVE

Poutine Pilgrimage Continued around the World

This is the second part of my poutine pilgrimage. I was, and continue to be, convinced that anyone can get poutine almost anywhere around the world today. When I think back to my days as an officer in the Canadian Army, it was close to impossible to find a poutine in Canada, let alone in other parts of the world. To prove it to myself and to fulfill the research for this book, I felt I needed to travel to different locations in search of poutine. In preparation, I came up with a set of guiding rules:

1) At least one location had to be in Canada outside of the province of Quebec because poutine is too well-known there;
2) At least two locations had to be in the United States, as American fast food is very much part of American culture;

3) One location had to be far away from Canada;
4) One location had to be in Europe, where food culture is very different.

I travel a great deal because of work and decided that I would use these opportunities to seek out poutine. I chose Toronto, Cleveland, New Orleans, Mooloolaba in Australia, and Lille in France. I was already headed to each of these cities, aside from Mooloolaba, to attend academic conferences. I had never to been Cleveland and I was curious to see how the city looks and feels. My second pick was New Orleans. It was far enough away and, because of the Acadian connection, visiting the Big Easy is well suited to a book on poutine. I was interested to see if New Orleans had embraced the dish.

The location in Europe was also an easy decision. France has a special connection with Quebec, so I believed it was important to evaluate any French connection through poutine. As for a location that was geographically distant from Quebec, you couldn't do much better than Australia. I took a map of Australia, closed my eyes, and randomly pointed to a spot, which turned out to be Mooloolaba, a town close to Brisbane.

The second step was to figure out how to pick the restaurant I would visit in each location. I again devised criteria to help choose my locations:

1) I could not pick a chain restaurant. The restaurant had to be independently owned, and the decisions around selling, preparing, and serving poutine had to be local.

2) I had to go to the hotel clerk to ask where I would find the best poutine in town. I wanted to confirm whether I needed to explain what poutine was and ensure that I visited a location they believed had great poutine. Of course, I took the risk of being sent to a restaurant that was not highly rated, but I would look at some websites before consulting to validate recommendations.
3) I wanted to arrive at the location when it wasn't busy so that I could talk to the people working there.
4) Once at the location, I had to ask the server to order for me what they thought was the best poutine.
5) I also had to eat some of the poutine but did not have to finish it.

I am not a restaurant critic, and I'd never done anything like this before. The rules I set made me feel comfortable. When I visit a restaurant, particularly for the first time, I never order off the menu. I always ask the server to order their favourite meal for me. It's something I've done for a long time. A restaurant will always serve you what they believe is the best dish as they want you to come back. The same approach with poutine seemed like a good plan. How hard could it be?

Poutine in Toronto

Toronto was my only Canadian stop on what was to be the international leg of my poutine pilgrimage. I wanted to see how Toronto, the most populous city in Canada, was handling Canada's newest iconic dish. Despite being the largest city in Canada, Toronto could appropriately be described as an international city. Consequently, it has struggled somewhat to develop its own identity. It has embraced the cultures of many other nations, but, as someone who doesn't live there, I cannot say what is different and unique about Toronto compared to other cities. One thing is for sure, though: in Toronto, poutine is served everywhere. While exploring Queen Street and other parts of the city, I found poutine on most restaurant menus.

While staying at a hotel downtown, I asked the concierge where the best place to eat a poutine was in Toronto. As the largest metropolitan area in Canada, surely it would have a few good places. At first, the concierge pointed to both Queen West and the Distillery District. But I insisted on being pointed in the direction of what was considered the *best* poutine in the city. The concierge took about fifteen minutes to look through recommendations and listen to their coworkers' anecdotes before saying one name: Poutini's. The name sounded like a cheap Italian restaurant, but I assumed the owner wanted a catchy name. Thanking the concierge for their help, I headed to Poutini's. Originally called Poutini's House of Poutine, it is located in downtown Toronto, but was abruptly shut down in 2017 after employees locked the door and posted a note saying that they had left because of unsafe working conditions. The restaurant has since changed ownership. The environment appears to be calm, at least during the day. At night I'm sure things become undoubtedly more interesting.

Photo 12.1. In front of Poutini's in Toronto, considered by many as the best place to eat poutine in Toronto.

I'd seen the name many times on various culinary websites about poutine in Toronto. As I taxied there, I was feeling quite confident that I had made the right choice. I was hungry and I was looking forward to a nice poutine à la Toronto. Poutini's is all about freshness for the sake of flavour, from hand-cut, skin-on fries to cheese from Maple Dale Farms, which is delivered every other day.

As I was getting closer, I could tell why Queen Street West has a reputation of offering diverse restaurants. It is filled with intriguing, unpretentious little eateries. It's nothing like Bay Street, Yorkville, or many places in Toronto you feel you can't afford as you enter. If I were living in Toronto and dating, Queen Street West would be a place I would spend some time.

The taxi driver had a hard time finding the actual place, questioning if I had the right address. I honestly was not sure if the place was closed or had moved. We continued looking around and eventually ended up finding a very dark front window with the words I was looking for: Poutini's. I paid the driver and walked over.

The restaurant was astonishingly simple and small, really small. Barely ten people could sit to eat inside the restaurant. The ordering counter was at the end of the restaurant, almost all in wood, a nice touch. The menu board was plastered with features like wings and other types of junk food, unrelated to poutine. I wondered, if this was the mecca of poutine in Toronto, how can the restaurant sell other dishes? After all, Poutini's was the self-proclaimed house of poutine.

I approached the counter and spoke to the cashier, Franco. I noticed he had a Spanish accent. After chatting a bit, I found out that his parents were from Ecuador, but he was born in raised in Canada. I asked him if he ate poutine regularly. He told me he did, and that he has enjoyed it since he was a kid. I asked him if he was serving the best poutine in the city. His response was unequivocally positive. He was proud to serve a Canadian traditional dish, he said. A Canadian dish … interesting. I asked him what poutine I should order, or which poutine is Poutini's best. His response was the traditional poutine: fries, gravy, and cheese curds. Great, let's go for it. It was seven dollars for a decent-sized portion, a bargain for Toronto.

After waiting for about eight minutes, I received my order of poutine. I picked it up at the counter, went back to my seat, and dug in. It was interestingly spicy, but the fries were undercooked, and the cheese curds were small, very small. It was sadly underwhelming, but I was hungry, so I ate it all. My expectations were not that high, even in Toronto, but still, I was in the house of poutine, Poutini's. It was not really what I was expecting. I honestly tried to forget my experience and moved on with my day.

Poutine in Cleveland

Cleveland, Ohio, was my second stop. Americans have a special relationship with fast food. It's everywhere, and it is embedded in their culture. It is difficult to avoid junk food when visiting the United States. I was looking forward to going to Cleveland as I had never been there. Based on some discussions I have had with colleagues, it's not well-known, and some suggested that the city was violent and not a great tourist destination. Cleveland's crime rate is very high, so my expectations flying into the city were very low. Cleveland is home to the ever-losing Cleveland Browns, the Cleveland Guardians baseball team, and the former NBA champions, the Cavaliers. Cleveland is also home of the Rock & Roll Hall of Fame, as the city claims to be its birthplace. Cleveland is also the setting for the popular sitcom *The Drew Carey Show*, which ran from 1995 to 2004. You hear about Cleveland every now and then, but it's not a place you often talk about as a place to visit. I was looking forward to visiting this city with no real identity, at least from what I knew.

Photo 12.2. In front of Local West, considered by many to be the best place to eat poutine in Cleveland.

I arrived on a beautiful Tuesday afternoon in June. The flights from Halifax to Toronto and then to Cleveland were uneventful. The heat was noticeable due to a warm breeze coming across the lake. Otherwise, it was sunny and beautiful, so I figured I would take a walk around and see the neighbourhood. Cleveland is a typical mid-sized city of four hundred thousand, with a beautiful downtown core filled with majestic buildings, such as the gem of the Rock & Roll Hall of Fame, and small parks. The architecture is diverse, from modern to Gothic and contemporary, but it works. The one thing I did notice was that there were lots of restaurants. Suburbia seemed close enough for people to bike or even walk into town to enjoy them.

The diverse immigrant communities in Cleveland each bring their own distinct culinary identity. This melting pot of culinary traditions creates a unique local cuisine. Examples of these are found in neighbourhoods such as Little Italy,

Photo 12.3. Poutine with parmesan powder and a wine-based sauce.

Slavic Village, and Tremont. I asked a few locals what Cleveland's best-known dish was, but I did not get much of an answer. As far as I could tell, Cleveland's blue-collar roots have influenced the food scene, making Cleveland's food culture modestly simple – perfect place to look for poutine. Looking online, I found that there were many places where I could eat poutine. The best rated spot in town was called Local West, on Detroit Avenue. I checked with the concierge downstairs and validated that it was a good place to go. He did, however, warn me of how rough the district was. I was not really concerned because I left the hotel at around 11 a.m., and it was a bright sunny day. He told me it would take about an hour to get there on foot. This was a great opportunity to see a city I knew very little about. By the time I got there, it would be about an hour before lunch time.

I crossed the Detroit–Superior Bridge to enter Cleveland's west side, and the weather soon became hot and muggy.

As I ventured down Detroit Avenue, I felt I was entering a different dimension, a more realistic aspect of Cleveland. There were abandoned cars, boarded windows, dirty streets, closed shops, and people hanging around. It was a rough part of town, and I was starting to think that maybe this was not a great idea. But I ventured on, and the street started to improve, with familiar chain restaurants and shops. I found Local West about a kilometre after I passed another well-known poutine place called Banter. It was at the corner of two streets. The inside was small; it could fit roughly thirty people. Unlike Banter, Local West has a small patio in the front. I briefly thought about entering Banter, but my goal was to try Local West's poutine.

As I entered, I noticed that the counter was at the far end of the restaurant. There were more people working than patrons in the restaurant. I could tell that the employees were preparing for a busy lunch period. I moved closer to the counter to look at the menu and saw different bottles of wine and beer for sale.

As I looked over the menu, I only found one poutine, the oddly named UB40 Poutine. So, I went to the counter to introduce myself and to place my order. The cashier's name was Emilia. She was the owner's niece. In fact, all four employees in the restaurant were related. Her uncle was the owner and cook and was standing a few feet away. He clearly was not the talking type. He said hello and continued his work in the kitchen. Most owners of places like this are shy, reserved, and don't deal well with the public. Emilia was more open and was all about customer service.

Photo 12.4. Inside Local West, in Cleveland, Ohio.

Emilia explained to me that the poutine name was inspired by wine. The gravy was wine based, named after UB40, the British band that covered Neil Diamond's 1967 song "Red, Red, Wine." Simple but cute. So, I ordered the poutine, US$14. Given that it was close to lunch time, it started to get busy so I couldn't talk much with Emilia, but I was able to ask her a few questions. I told her that the hotel I was staying at recommended that I come here for a poutine, and I asked her why she believed a hotel would do that. She said that many people from across town come to Local West to try their poutine. I also asked her about Banter, the restaurant next door that also sold poutine. She claimed that while Banter was a good place for poutine, their poutine was the best. Can't knock her for lack of confidence.

Poutine is alive and well in Ohio and many other states. Poutine is even used as a reference point to describe new dishes now. In Iowa, to describe a new type of hamburger, a reporter made a reference to poutine in an article.[1] That's a clear indication that poutine is known in many parts of America.

While I waited for my order, the restaurant began to fill up with more clientele. People ordered, and as their orders arrived, I noted that they were mostly sandwiches and fries – no poutines. Emilia came over with my poutine after a short wait. I looked at it. It took me a bit to recognize what cheese I was looking at. Finally, I realized that the dish was sprinkled with parmesan cheese. No cheese curds! The fries had some peelings, which seems typical now. The bowl was a decent-sized serving, so I couldn't complain about that, but my first bite was weird. The sauce was something I had never tasted before. I could tell there was wine in it, but my Quebecer palate was telling me that the combination was wrong. The parmesan made me feel more desperate for cheese, any cheese really, not just curds. It was an underwhelming experience. I couldn't eat the whole thing.

I went back to Emilia to thank her and told her I was full. I asked her if many people ordered the dish. She told me it was one of their most popular dishes on the menu. I wondered what the customers would have thought if they tried a poutine in Quebec with cheese curds.

Poutine and the Big Easy, New Orleans

My third stop was New Orleans. My French Canadian roots brought me to the Big Easy. New Orleans is a fascinating

Photo 12.5. Cajun poutine, New Orleans's style.

place, a place of celebration, where poverty meets wealth in a symbiotic fashion. There is no place like it, at least not in America. New Orleans is a mixture between Amsterdam and a decent-sized town in the United States, like Milwaukee or Green Bay. You forget you're in America, sometimes. The French culture is everywhere, for obvious reasons. The effects of "Le grand dérangement," the deportation of French-speaking Acadians from the Maritime provinces of Canada, is still quite present. Most street names are French, and in some places, it appears to be more French than Montreal. It is a special place indeed. I always enjoy going to New Orleans. This time I was on the hunt for a poutine à la Cajun.

I was intrigued to see how poutine would fit in New Orleans. The city's white-linen tablecloths are graced by crawfish étouffée, whether in a bistro courtyard or along Bourbon Street, where it's always loud. People eat bowls of gumbo and po-boy sandwiches stuffed with fried oysters on picnic benches. It's a spicy, tasty fusion between creole cuisine, Cajun cuisine, and soul food. Food there is as festive as it is elegant, in a curious way. Poutine, with its French

Photo 12.6. With Miguel and David from Mexico, enjoying a poutine in New Orleans, Cajun style.

Canadian origin and humble mix of affordable ingredients, seemed like it would fit right in.

While at my hotel, I began my search for the perfect place to try poutine. As before, I asked the hotel concierge where to find the best poutine in town. At first, she was not sure what I was talking about. As I began to describe the dish, she understood what I meant. She recommended that I go to the French Quarter and suggested Chez Amélie, a cute bistro with a garden. It wasn't the typical french fry joint you would find elsewhere in the United States. But she mentioned that they serve poutine, the authentic version. So off I went.

It was a Monday night, and it was very hot and muggy, thirty-five degrees. I was walking on Royal Street, which runs parallel to Bourbon Street. On my way to the restaurant, I got into the New Orleans spirit. The restaurant was about two kilometres from my hotel. It was nice to walk around and absorb the atmosphere. Unfortunately, when I got to the restaurant, I found that it was closed on Mondays. I knew what I was doing the following day.

On my return to Chez Amélie, it was open and busy. The hotel told me a reservation was not necessary, but that's

Photo 12.7. Outside Chez Émilie's, in New Orleans.

exactly what they asked. As I was on my own, they gladly showed me to the bar inside, where it was much cooler. The patio was gorgeous, with a beautiful fountain. I could see many small tables with white tablecloths and lanterns with actual fire, which is typical in New Orleans. There were no kids, just couples. I was seated at the bar, which had five or six stools. I joined one gentleman who was sitting at the bar but chatted with the bartender.

I was given the menu for drinks and food. I asked the bartender if they served poutine. She said they did. I replied that I was from Canada and would love to try the poutine. She whispered to me that the poutine they had was not the same as what I would find in Canada. She was clearly apologetic about it. The poutine was US$12. A bit expensive for a simple dish, but I was in the French Quarter, so most things were expensive.

My goal was to find out how the famous dish from Quebec survived its trek to the Big Easy. The poutine they had was called "Cajun style," so I was a little surprised that it wasn't the Acadian-style poutine, which is more of a dumpling. Many Acadians migrated to Louisiana years ago, but perhaps the Acadian-style poutine never made the transition. I could tell that not very many would order a poutine at this café, given the fame of various Cajun dishes. Poutine only entered restaurants' menus likely because of Acadians and French settlers. This led me to ask my server, Julia, about Acadian-style poutine, and she had no idea what I was talking about or whether it was on the menu.

As I was waiting, two gentlemen from out of town joined me at the bar. Miguel and David were from Mexico City, in New Orleans for pleasure. Coincidentally, they were in the business of ingredient supply, providing fructose to companies in the United States. They both had been to Canada several times, so they knew the country, Toronto mostly. They also knew what poutine was, but they had never ordered it. They mentioned that they disliked Italian food in Canada and avoided Mexican food at all costs, for fear of being disappointed. I found it interesting that they were complaining about the heat, coming from a warm climate. I told them that I was from Canada, and that I, too, was melting from the heat. We talk about food trends and what was going on in Mexico. Of course, there was one topic we couldn't avoid: Trump. As I was talking with them, I realized that we had a lot in common – similar struggles as both nations were trying to contribute to the world while being overshadowed by the United States. I could feel their frustration.

Midway through our conversation, my order of poutine arrived. It was in a bowl, a good portion, but not too overwhelming. It consisted of fries with the peel, some gravy, pulled pork, buttered sautéed onions, and melted cheese, not cheese curds. Not the classic picture I had in mind, but it was clearly New Orleans style. It had a little kick to it.

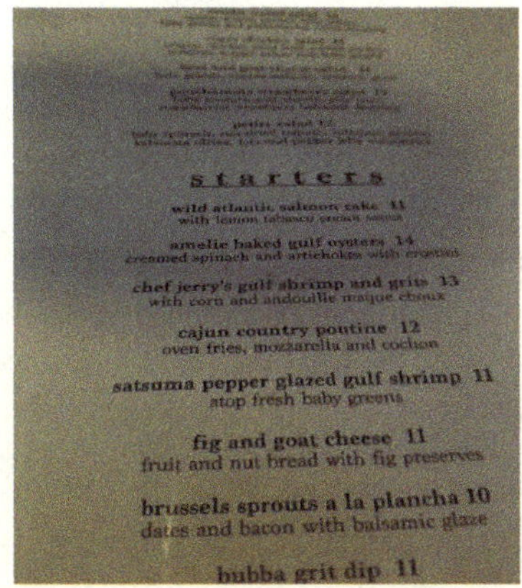

Photo 12.8. Cajun country poutine on the menu.

Every bite was spicy, and the mixture between the ingredients was interesting. It was not overly filling, either. I finished in less than ten minutes as I was talking to Miguel and David. They had the jambalaya. Overall, the poutine was a nice pause from a hot muggy day in New Orleans, but it was not a dish I would write home about.

I wanted to walk around town before heading back to the hotel, so I said goodbye to my new friends and left. As I was walking back to the hotel on Bourbon Street, I watched people listening to loud music and strangers talking to each other. It was then that I started to notice signs of decay in the human fabric of the city. There were people sleeping everywhere and potholes in the street; it was clear that the city was struggling. All I could think of was Katrina, the devastating hurricane that hit New Orleans in 2005. The city is still trying to get back on its feet. The next morning, while jogging in the city to burn off all the calories from my poutine, I saw at least twenty rats roaming Bourbon Street. Sad, but I hope the city will come back. It's just an incredible place that looks like an ongoing social experiment. You can see things you wouldn't see elsewhere in America, and it is difficult not to care about New Orleans. It needs to survive. America needs New Orleans more than it needs America.

Poutine in the Land Down Under

My fourth stop was Mooloolaba, Australia. I picked Australia as it is on the other side of the planet from Quebec, and chose Mooloolaba by pointing at a map with my eyes closed. The entire trip from Halifax takes roughly thirty-two hours, and twenty-six hours of it is in flight. It was quite the trek! After three flights, two buses, and a taxi, I finally arrived at my destination.

Mooloolaba is a resort town in the state of Queensland, with many hotels and restaurants, and a gorgeous, endless beach. This was my fourth visit to Australia, but it was my first time on the Sunshine Coast. It was different from Sydney, very different. I quickly noticed that most people walking around were seniors. This worried me as fast-food joints and poutine generally reflect youth, university students, and an active nightlife. I arrived at my hotel, got settled in, and despite the long journey, I wanted to visit the town and find poutine. As usual, I went to the front desk to ask where I could find poutine. The desk clerk knew what poutine was and immediately looked for a place online. Lo and behold, there was a place, two blocks away. It was called the Goodbar. A simple name.

Photo 12.9. Me and poutine in Australia.

It was a beautiful day, twenty-five degrees, not a cloud in sight. Goodbar was a pub located at the corner of a residential area. There was a patio in front, almost as big as the restaurant. Inside it was dark, even with all the doors open. There were one or two couples sitting inside. It was in the middle of the afternoon, so I was not surprised to find it quiet in the bar. The place was set up for trivia night, with large higher tables for groups to compete against each other.

I walked in and asked the server, Bailey, for a menu. The menu stated that the poutine was served with gravy, onions, and real cheese curds for AUS$12. I was immediately impressed. I asked Bailey if many people ordered poutine, and she told me that it was one of their most popular dishes. She also mentioned that people tended to order it in the afternoon, to share, or late in the evening with beer or alcohol. I told her that I was Canadian, and she said she

Photo 12.10. The poutine at Goodbar in Mooloolaba, near Brisbane in Australia.

knew poutine came from Canada. She didn't encourage me to order anything else, so I ordered the poutine.

As we were waiting for the dish, we chatted about school, life, and travel. Bailey was about to leave for Europe in a few days as she wanted to see the world. She had no idea when she would come back, but she told me she would. It could be six months, a year, she did not know. Australians tend to do that. The continent is so isolated from the rest of the world that many feel the urge to leave and discover the world. Australians are as intrigued by the world as the world is by Australia. Most Australians have a passport and are well-travelled. When travelling, you discover different cuisines, traditions, and tastes. This may explain why poutine is made and sold in Australia. Poutine has the distinct quality of being easy to remember when you encounter it for the first time. The recipe appears simple. Again, these qualities have likely helped the dish become so famous.

The poutine arrived in an oval bowl. The portion was a good size, not too big. The fries had peel, and the cheese was melted. Surprisingly, the dish had real cheese curds, made in Victoria. I did not expect to find curds in Australia. The taste was not bad at all, and the cheese made all the difference. It was surprisingly good. Even the gravy was hearty, a beef broth that made the whole dish work. The fries were a little crispy, which made the blending between all of the ingredients more enjoyable. While I did not want to spoil my dinner by eating the whole dish, I did anyway.

After I was done, I went over to the kitchen to speak to the cook. His name was Guy, and he was from Brisbane. He had spent some time in Canada, so he knew very well what poutine was. He apologized to me as he knew the kind of poutine I was accustomed to eating. I told him it was likely one of the best poutines I have eaten outside Canada, outside Quebec for that matter. Guy was very pleased as he was not sure how it would stack up. I mentioned to him that I was surprised to find cheese curds in my poutine in Australia. He showed me the bag of curds and explained where the manufacturing plant was located. He also mentioned that most poutine in Australia is served with curds. Guy told me that there were many good places in Brisbane that served poutine. He was almost nostalgic about it. He said Australians are generally very familiar with the Canadian dish and like to share it with friends. If it's not nachos, it's poutine, especially during the winter months.

I thanked both Bailey and Guy for the company and left. I walked around town to see what was on other restaurants' menus. Most restaurants were along the beach. However, pubs like the Goodbar were to be found more in the residential areas. It was a pleasant afternoon altogether, and I left with the impression that the land down under had a love affair with poutine that had started a long time ago. Poutine was not even sixty years old, and the dish reached one of the farthest countries in the world. Just amazing to see.

Photo 12.11. Goodbar's menu.

Poutine in France

My visit to Lille, in France, was brief but very interesting. Lille is well-known for its agri-food sector, making it a fitting place for my poutine pilgrimage. I flew in early on a Thursday morning to deliver a keynote at a global protein summit about the future of protein. There is quite a divisive debate about producing protein from livestock or plants taking place these days, and I'm not sure it will disappear anytime soon. Vegans appear to be more vocal than ever before.

Lille is not only the capital of the Huts-de-France Region in northern France, but it is also a cultural hub with a very active university. While there were a few people from the United States and Canada, most of the people going to the conference were from Europe, which is why I was surprised to have been asked to deliver a keynote at the summit. Most surprising of all, I was asked to deliver a keynote in English, in France, as a French Canadian. While I was surprised, I was nevertheless excited to do so.

Photo 12.12. In front of P'tite Poutine in Lille, France.

My work is known in Canada, at least in the agri-food sector, but not in Europe. Europe is known for its heterogeneous food market; North America seems more homogeneous and is always catching up with research and data. Space is so abundant in Canada and the United States that we barely see problems before Europeans do. Plant-based dieting is driven by concerns around climate change, animal welfare, and of course health. It was the fourteenth annual summit. I remember, in 2005, during the first summit, we were barely talking about veganism in Canada.

In fact, while we were living in Regina in 2006, we hired our first nanny, Marla. At this point we had barely heard the term vegan. During her interview, Marla asked us if it was okay that she was a vegan. My wife and I both wondered what a vegan was and what they ate. As she became more acquainted with the family, it became obvious that she was separating from the family during mealtimes just because she had a different diet, which we found frustrating. In order to make mealtime more inclusive, we tried to become more involved in veganism. To my surprise, it was quite fulfilling. Since then, my view of different diets has been quite open. And honestly, I find these diets fascinating. It's the future really – how else can the industry transform and grow? By recognizing these dietary differences, we can better serve consumers and the planet at the same time. When I was done with my keynote, I was asked countless times if I was vegan. I suspect they have rarely had a non-vegan speaker before. I mean, steaks were not an option at the summit, it was clear. Someone was upset at the summit when they saw honey at the table where tea and coffee were provided. That's how sensitive the crowd was.

After the summit, I had some time to wander around town. It was in October and the weather was cool. Everyone was dressed up like it was in the middle of January. As a Canadian, I thought the weather was just perfect for a walk, even with the rain. I immediately thought of my poutine pilgrimage. I'd had poutine in many different places, but not in Europe, and France has a special place in the hearts of Canadians, especially Quebecers.

There are Canadians who believe poutine came from Europe and even France. Another reason this book is important to set the record straight. A visit to a poutine place in France was most appropriate. As usual, I went down to the front desk of the hotel to ask for a recommendation of the best place for poutine in Lille. Like so many times before, no explanation was required, and I was recommended a place called La P'tite Poutine, on Basse Street. It was not too far

Photo 12.13. Poutine in France with cheese curds made in Quebec.

from the hotel, about two kilometres away. I added a stop to my city walking tour.

The place was easy to find, decorated with Canada's and Quebec's flags. The business logo had moose antlers on it, playing to those cultural stereotypes. I could tell that the owners wanted to promote the Canadian brand. It looked to be a very small restaurant from the front, but it had a second floor where people could sit and eat their poutine. I arrived at around 2 p.m., which was perfect timing for me to talk with the staff.

The place felt Canadian. As I walked in, I met the owners, Clément and Frédéric. Both were wearing plaid shirts,

Photo 12.14. Me, Clément and Frédéric.

and Frédéric was wearing a Montreal Canadiens cap. They had a television set with Radio-Canada on. They had beer from Quebec for sale. I could tell the owners had done their homework to be able to depict a quintessential Canadian atmosphere. I mostly spoke to Clément when I was there as Frédéric was busy serving customers.

Clément told me they served 150 to 160 poutines a day. That was all they sold. Poutine is available elsewhere in Lille, but they owned the only place where poutine was the only thing on the menu. For the most part, people dropped by out of pure curiosity. They wanted to try the poutine they'd heard about. Clément had spent two years in Montreal working for a marketing firm before coming back to his hometown, Lille. Frédéric, on the other hand, had always lived in Lille. Neither was a trained chef or went to cooking school. In the restaurant, they basically had rudimentary cooking stoves. Nothing sophisticated. They had a third partner, but he was much less involved. Both were quite jovial and high-spirited. While I was there, a few customers came in to order poutine. One bought a poutine to go, with the gravy on the side, while others ventured to the dining room upstairs. Customers were either on their own or showed up in pairs. What was striking was how fit everyone was. One came in with a suit. He was clearly looking for a quick lunch between meetings. That's when I noticed the location and the restaurant's opening hours.

The restaurant was close to high-end stores in a very touristy place. Not what you would expect from a restaurant like this. It also closed at 10 p.m. In the majority of the cities I have been to, people eat poutine after going out to a bar or dancing. Yet at La P'tite Poutine, most of the business was during the day, which appeared to be working for them. They had only been open since June 2019. That day, while I was there, they sold at least twenty poutines in the middle of the afternoon. I was impressed.

This is France, so we obviously needed to talk about cooking and how the gravy and fries were prepared. The gravy was beef-based, which is typical, and they don't make anything different from what Clément experienced in Montreal. The fries were a different story. Everything was better. They served potatoes from the region, fresh and fried in vegetable oil, which was not surprising. Clément told me that in Lille they took fries very seriously, and it showed when I tried their poutine.

They had a very simple menu, with three different kinds of poutine. Three of them you could find anywhere. There was the classic, and bacon and sausages, but the one that intrigued me was called Ch'ti Poutine, which had sautéed onions and beer-marinated beef. The poutine was seven euros, which I thought was inexpensive. To my shock, I realized they were using cheese curds made in Quebec, by Fromagerie St-Guillaume. The curds made all the difference.

This very fromagerie had contacted me when they heard I was writing a book on poutine and told me that they had started to sell their cheese in France. So, it was here!

When I received my serving, I was surprised by the amount of cheese. I could barely see the fries and beef. It was incredibly appetizing. I could smell the spices and the onions as well. After the first few bites, I was absolutely overwhelmed – the poutine I was having in France tasted very much like poutine in Quebec. It was the best I have had outside of Quebec, full stop. They clearly had done their homework, and it paid off.

As I was saying goodbye, we took a few photos. I hope their business flourishes. They both have great spirits. It was interesting to see Europe, and especially France, steal a recipe from the "New World."

CHAPTER THIRTEEN

The Future of Poutine

We all face a dilemma when consuming and purchasing food. Often, we minimize the potential health impacts of junk food or fast food and try to offset negative health outcomes by reframing these "treats" as part of a healthy lifestyle – everything in moderation. One way of minimizing the potential harm is to emphasize the role of biological determinism, rather than behaviour and lifestyle, in governing health outcomes.[1] In other words, health outcomes are determined by genetics, and individuals and their choices don't influence lifestyle and health conditions.[2] Some research on biological determinism suggests that we want to indulge because we are naturally hard-wired to do so.[3] Our environment and our genetics dictate what we need and what we eat, suggesting that we don't have much control over our own nutritional destiny.

It's an interesting theory, but in the end, we are human beings. Food is a complicated issue, and it's impossible to pinpoint reasons why food choices are made. Fast food is still here, it is still part of our society, and it is highly unlikely that governments will ban it. It is part of who we are, what we do, and how we reward ourselves. In modern society, food intellectuals advocate for the perfect diet, free of fast food and anything that could make us less healthy. This obsession with food perfection is making some of us feel guilty about what we eat and want to eat.

Regardless, poutine won't disappear any time soon, as we enjoy indulging out taste buds and cravings. It's the dilemma we face every day. That choice is not necessarily health versus indulgence, but rather being human versus leading a life of food perfectionism.

Poutine is not a light meal, but it can be. It's not for those looking for a quick food-fix or a way to get healthier. With diets and trends, some food products tend to disappear and not survive the next generation. Poutine was invented more than a generation ago. But today's market is very different from that in 1957. Today, consumers make food choices based on a variety of factors: price, freshness, quality, convenience, health attributes, portability, ethics, and many more. Despite health-oriented dietary trends that could affect poutine's demand, the dish is more popular than ever.

Food habits have always undergone profound changes owing to social, economic, and technological transformations. Many recent studies show an increase in diets high in animal proteins, especially in consumers with low levels of education.[4] Consumers with a higher level of education tend to reduce the amount of meat consumed. For the younger generation, the importance of convenience foods emerges, mainly among couples but also among families with children. Busy lifestyles and different priorities give eating out more prominence and popularity. But new research is also noting how the market is becoming more heterogeneous when it comes to eating. New dietary sensitivities lead niches of consumers to choose healthier foods for better lifestyles. The market is changing very quickly, which is something we have not seen before.

The history of food consumption in Canada shows that our market is going through many transitions. Food consumption in Canada has changed rapidly over the last twenty years. In the 1950s and 1960s, when poutine arrived on the market, a period of rapid economic expansion, during which consumption rose dramatically, significantly influenced dietary patterns.[5] Convenience foods represent an expanding sector of the food industry, responding to a contemporary social demand for streamlined meal preparation.[6] Since the 1990s, health and safety concerns have become pivotal in purchasing food products. This understanding of health has become especially pertinent in the food industry and has gained enormous potency as far as consumer choice is concerned. These trends are even more perceivable in recent years.

But food skills and food literacy are real. Research indicates that child participation in Canadian household food-related activities is not as significant as it used to be. Children are not as involved in choosing meals, grocery shopping, and meal preparation as in the past.[7] And we don't expect that trend to change in the years to come. Demographic differences are often observed between region, education level, and Indigenous and immigration status. As these trends impact how we consume food, demand for fast food and less healthy options will change. As poutine is inherently associated with the fast-food market, we expect that some groups are more exposed to fast food than others.[8]

The other reality affecting younger generations is access to home ownership. Often called "generation rent," an increasing number of consumers do not want to commit to buying a home. More and more young people are also living in private rentals "for longer periods of their lives because they are unable to access homeownership or social housing."[9] Many young people feel frustrated as they struggle to find a permanent home. This phenomenon is happening in many parts of the world, including Canada. As a result, some studies suggest that future generations will become more nomadic and will travel even more than former generations. With food consumption, the fact that we'll have more consumers who are transient may affect their ability to cook and settle down. It is easy to speculate how fast food and poutine can only gain in popularity.

Since prices are so high, some developers are trying to make home ownership more affordable. In Toronto, they are now selling condos without full kitchens.[10] Kitchens were always considered the heart of the home, but younger generations will see more homes without them, as the kitchen's role is changing. With less space or less opportunity to own a permanent home, technology and access to food is also going to be a key factor for the younger generations. Food-delivery applications and meal kits will become more influential.[11] UBS, a well-known consulting firm, estimates that the global online food ordering market could grow to over $400 billion by 2030.[12] Delivery and poutine are not overly compatible concepts, unlike other fast-food fixes like pizza or fried chicken. Poutine will need to find a way to stay relevant. This is likely poutine's greatest menace for the future. Poutine's most significant strength is its socializing ability. With technology, the connection between people and food can weaken, thus not allowing for any socializing to occur.[13]

Whether poutine will be compatible with the needs and wants of future generations remains to be seen. Poutine's popularity was elevated by the rise of fast food and its availability. On any given day, one Canadian in seven will eat fast food purchased from a restaurant chain. Countless studies have shown how fast food is not a healthy choice and can lead to chronic diseases. Adding poutine to the menu only gave the dish more attention. Children and teenagers tend to enjoy fast food, particularly burgers and soft drinks, more than other demographics, but the health of many has been affected as a result. They prefer fast food primarily for the delicious taste, followed by convenience.[14]

Poutine does have a future, but it must continue to adapt to different tastes and styles. Poutine, like other fast-food solutions, is malleable and can survive several trends.

Acknowledgments

Bringing *Poutine Nation* to life has been a journey filled with insight, collaboration, and unwavering support. I would like to extend my deepest gratitude to the incredible team at University of Toronto Press, particularly Jennifer, Josephine, and Jessica. Your dedication, expertise, and enthusiasm have been instrumental in shaping this book, and I am truly grateful for your contributions. Thank you for believing in this project and for your commitment to sharing its story with readers. Your efforts have made all the difference.

Appendix

Person	Role played in poutine's elevation
Jean-Guy Lainesse	First creator of original poutine
Fernand and Germaine Lachance	Father and mother of original poutine
Jean-Paul Roy	Inventor of modern poutine
Ashton Leblond	Godfather of poutine
Jean-Louis Roy	Poutine's premier ambassador in Canada
Ryan Smolkin	Poutine's premier ambassador globally

Chronology

Based on the research and evidence collected, here is a chronology of events, as I understand them:

Year	Event
1957	Jean-Guy Lainesse, a customer, asks Le Restaurant Café Idéal's owner in Warwick, Fernand Lachance, to mix fries and cheese together. Lachance coins the term "poutine" as he serves the first original poutine. The word "poutine" appears on a menu for the first time.
1962	Le Lutin Qui Rit Restaurant (formerly The Restaurant Café Idéal in Warwick) sells sauce as a side order, with fries and cheese curds. The sauce is made by Germaine Lettre Lachance, Fernand Lachance's wife.
1964	Jean-Paul Roy serves first modern poutine as we know it today (with fries, cheese curds and sauce), in a special container.

1972 Ashton Leblond, owner of Chez Ashton, introduces poutine on the restaurant's menu.

1980 Chez Ashton expands, becomes first multi-site restaurant chain to have poutine on its menu.

1987 A Quebec City-based Burger King franchise owner in Drummondville, Jean-Louis Roy, is given permission to add poutine to its menu.

1988 Burger King allows all its franchise owners in Quebec and in Hawkesbury to sell poutine.

1990 McDonald's adds poutine to its menu throughout the province of Quebec.

1992 Harvey's sells poutine across the country, becoming the first country-wide restaurant chain to sell poutine.

1998 Daniel Leblanc, the new Roy Jucep owner, receives a certificate, issued by the Canadian Intellectual Property Office, claiming that Jean-Paul Roy in Drummondville is the "inventor of poutine."

2007 CBC ranks poutine as Canada's tenth greatest invention.

2008 Smoke's Poutinerie, founded by Ryan Smolkin and the first specialty chain solely focused on selling poutine, opens first restaurant.

2013 McDonald's adds poutine to its menus across Canada.

2016 Poutine is served at the White House in Washington, DC, during an official state dinner.

2017 *McLean's* magazine ranks poutine as Canada's #1 iconic food.

2017 Smoke's Poutinerie opens 150th store.

2018 Smoke's Poutinerie opens stores in California, Florida, and Dubai.

Notes

Introduction

1 C. Fortin, "Trois activités antiblues," *Chatelaine* 49, no. 2 (2008): 22; J. Coulon, "Le Printemps dans Chaudière-Appalaches," *Actualité Médicale* 26, no. 11 (2005): 59–61.

2 Blog of Lists, "7 Surprising Facts About Poutine," *Maclean's*, August 15, 2012, https://www.macleans.ca/society/life/7-surprising-facts-about-poutine/.

3 Louis Roy and Michel Verdon, "East-Farnham's Agriculture in 1871: Ethnicity, Circumstances, and Economic Rationale in Quebec's Eastern Townships," *The Canadian Historical Review* 84, no. 3 (September): 355–93, https://doi.org/10.3138/CHR.84.3.355.

4 S. Stender, J. Dyerberg, and A. Astrup, "Fast Food: Unfriendly and Unhealthy," *International Journal of Obesity* 31, no. 6 (July 2007): 887–90, https://doi.org/10.1038/sj.ijo.0803616.

5 Nicholas Fabien-Ouellet, "Poutine, Mezcal and Hard Cider: The Making of Culinary Identities in North America" (PhD diss., University of Vermont, 2017), https://scholarworks.uvm.edu/graddis/805/.

6 Vanessa Lu, "McDonald's Serves Up Quebec Comfort Food," *Toronto Star*, December 6, 2013, S10.

7 Suman Roy and Brooke Ali, *From Pemmican to Poutine: A Journey Through Canada's Culinary History* (Key Publishing House, 2010).

8 Bruce Kraig and Colleen Taylor Sen, eds., *Street Food Around the World: An Encyclopedia of Food and Culture* (Abc-clio, 2013).

9 Bula Tibbitts and Morrow Corey, "Cultural Systems for Growing Potatoes in Space," *Acta Horticulturae* 230 (1988): 287–9, https://doi.org/10.17660/ActaHortic.1988.230.36.
10 Nik L.M. Grubben and Karel J. Keesman, "Modelling Ventilated Bulk Storage of Agromaterials: A Review," *Computers and Electronics in Agriculture* 114 (June 2015): 285–95, https://doi.org/10.1016/j.compag.2015.04.011.
11 Carole Paradis and Darlene Lacharité, "Apparent Phonetic Approximation: English Loanwords in Old Quebec French," *Journal of Linguistics* 44, no. 1 (2008): 87–128, https://doi.org/10.1017/S0022226707004963.
12 Lauren Pelley, "Poutine Inventions Offer New Wheys to Eat Your Curds," *Toronto Star*, 2015, E1.
13 "Poutine: Finally, a Definition," *Canadian Living*, May 21, 2014, https://www.canadianliving.com/food/article/poutine-finally-a-definition.
14 Radio-Canada, *Appels trompeurs: La liste des comtés s'allonge, l'opposition réclame une enquête indépendante* (Canadian Broadcasting Corporation, 2012).
15 The Canadian Press, "Who is Pierre Poutine?," *Maclean's*, August 14, 2014, https://web.archive.org/web/20230327075939/www.macleans.ca/politics/ottawa/who-is-pierre-poutine/; Dan Bilefsky, "Calling Poutine 'Canadian' Gives Some in Quebec Indigestion," *New York Times*, December 19, 2017, https://www.nytimes.com/2017/12/19/world/canada/quebec-poutine.html.
16 Caroline Durand, review of *Maudite poutine! L'histoire approximative d'un plat populaire* by Charles-Alexandre Théorêt, avec la collaboration d'Ève Derome et de Raphaël Martin, *Cuizine* 1, no. 2 (2009), https://doi.org/10.7202/037862ar.

2. Poutine?!

1 Alan Gordon, "Teaching Quebec: Why Quebec's History Matters to English Canada," *Canadian Issues* (2013): 47–50.
2 Hazem Rasheed Gaber and Len Tiu Wright, "Fast Food Advertising in Social Media: A Case Study on Facebook in Egypt," *The Business & Management Review* 5, no. 1 (June 2014): 91.
3 S. Krashinsky, "A Code for Inspiration," *Globe and Mail* (Index-Only), 2014, L6.

3. What Is Poutine, Really?

1 Sheryl Ubelacker, "Poutine Going Mainstream South of the Border; Quebec's Signature Concoction of Fries, Cheese Curds and Gravy is Showing Up on American Menus," *Toronto Star*, January 20, 2010, E7.
2 Robert J. Hyde and Steven A. Witherly, "Dynamic Contrast: A Sensory Contribution to Palatability," *Appetite* 21, no. 1 (August 1993): 1–16, https://doi.org/10.1006/appe.1993.1032.

3 Adam Leith Gollner, "Quebec's Baddest Poutine – For the Richest, Runniest, Gut-Busting-Est Combo of Fries, Cheese and Gravy, Head to Its Canadian Birthplace," *Wall Street Journal*, May 3, 2014, D9, https://www.wsj.com/articles/SB10001424052702303834304579521780148435834.

4 Daniel St-Gelais, Jean Lessard, Claude P. Champagne, and Jean-Christophe Vuillemard, "Production of Fresh Cheddar Cheese Curds with Controlled Postacidification and Enhanced Flavour," *Journal of Dairy Science* 92, no. 5 (May 2009): 1856–63, https://doi.org/10.3168/jds.2008-1761.

5 Daniel St-Gelais, Jean Lessard, Claude P. Champagne, et al., "Production of Fresh Cheddar."

6 Doug Gloin, "Say Cheese, Then Make It Happen; Keen Students Gather for Workshop From Feta to Cheddar, It Was an Adventure," *Toronto Star*, February 2, 2005, D12.

7 June Chua, "On a Quest to Bring Real Poutine to Berlin," *Toronto Star*, March 1, 2017, E6.

8 P.A. Swearingen, D.E. Adams, and T.L. Lensmire, "Factors Affecting Calcium Lactate and Liquid Expulsion Defects in Cheddar Cheese," *Journal of Dairy Science* 87, no. 3 (April 2004): 574–82, https://doi.org/10.3168/jds.S0022-0302(04)73199-9.

9 Fabien-Ouellet, "Poutine, Mezcal and Hard Cider," 27.

10 Carole E. Lee, "Canadian Prime Minister to Visit White House; Justin Trudeau is Expected to Discuss Economic Cooperation and Other Issues with President Barack Obama," *Wall Street Journal*, March 9, 2016, https://www.wsj.com/articles/canadian-prime-minister-to-visit-white-house-1457580501.

11 Máirtín Mac Con Iomaire and Pádraic Óg Gallagher, "The Potato in Irish Cuisine and Culture," *Journal of Culinary Science & Technology* 7, nos. 2–3 (2009): 152–67, https://doi.org/10.1080/15428050903313457.

12 Peter H. Argersinger, review of *Our Common Country: Family Farming, Culture, and Community in the Nineteenth-Century Midwest* by Susan Sessions Rugh," *Rural History* 13, no. 2 (October 2002): 253–59, https://doi.org/10.1017/S0956793302240145

13 *Wikipedia, The Free Encyclopedia*, s.v. "Potato," accessed June 20, 2025, https://en.wikipedia.org/wiki/Potato.

14 *Wikipedia*, "Potato."

15 David A. Ramírez, Jan Kreuze, Walter Amoros, et al., "Extreme Salinity as a Challenge to Grow Potatoes Under Mars-Like Soil Conditions: Targeting Promising Genotypes," *International Journal of Astrobiology* 18, no. 1 (February 2019): 18–24, https://doi.org/10.1017/S1473550417000453.

16 *Wikipedia*, "Potato."

17 Emily Monaco, "Can Belgium Claim Ownership of the French Fry?" *BBC Travel*, July 31, 2018.

18 "Our History," *McCain*, accessed May 7, 2025, https://www.mccain.com/about-us/our-history/.

19 "Poutine Québécois," *Cook's Info*, last updated March 31, 2021, https://www.cooksinfo.com/poutine-quebecoise.

20 Glenn Alderson, "RANGE Magazine's Guide to Quebec City," *Range*, July 3, 2024, https://readrange.com/range-guide-to-quebec-city/.
21 Poutineville, "Menu Poutineville Montreal," 2023, https://poutineville.com/en/menu/montreal/.
22 Remo Zaccagna, "Donair Voted Halifax's Official Food," *Chronicle Herald*, December 9, 2015, A3.
23 CBC News, "Small Quebec Town Breaks World Record for Largest Poutine," *CBC News*, August 3, 2019, https://www.cbc.ca/news/canada/montreal/world-record-for-largest-poutine-1.5235756.

4. Why the First Time You Eat Poutine Matters

1 Patricia Pliner and Paul Rozin, "The Psychology of the Meal," in *Dimensions of the Meal: The Science, Culture, Business, and Art of Eating*, ed. Herbert L. Meiselman (Aspen Publishers, 2000), quoted in Elizabeth Rode, Paul Rozin, and Paula Durlach, "Experienced and Remembered Pleasure for Meals: Duration Neglect but Minimal Peak, End (Recency) or Primacy Effects," *Appetite* 49, no. 1 (July 2007): 18–29, https://doi.org/10.1016/j.appet.2006.09.006.
2 Rode, Rozin, and Durlach, "Experienced and Remembered Pleasure," 18–29.
3 Marcel Adam Just, Vladimir L. Cherkassky, Sandesh Aryal, and Tom M. Mitchell, "A Neurosemantic Theory of Concrete Noun Representation Based on the Underlying Brain Codes (Neurosemantic Theory)," *PLoS One* 5, no. 1 (January 2010): E8622, https://doi.org/10.1371/journal.pone.0008622.
4 "Eating What's Good for You," *The Futurist*, 1998, 9.
5 Katrijn Houben, Fania C.M. Dassen, and Anita Jansen, "Taking Control: Working Memory Training in Overweight Individuals Increases Self-Regulation of Food Intake," *Appetite* 105 (October 2016): 567–74, https://doi.org/10.1016/j.appet.2016.06.029.
6 Teiko Suto, Kenichi Meguro, Masahiro Nakatsuka, et al., "Disorders of 'Taste Cognition' are Associated with Insular Involvement in Patients with Alzheimer's Disease and Vascular Dementia: 'Memory of Food is Impaired in Dementia and Responsible for Poor Diet,'" *International Psychogeriatrics* 26, no. 7 (July 2014): 1127–38, https://doi.org/10.1017/S1041610214000532.
7 Danielle Ferriday, Matthew L. Bosworth, Samantha Lai, et al., "Effects of Eating Rate on Satiety: A Role for Episodic Memory?," *Physiology & Behavior* 152, pt. B (December 2015): 389–96, https://doi.org/10.1016/j.physbeh.2015.06.038.
8 Amir Heiman and Oded Lowengart, "The Calorie Dilemma: Leaner and Larger, or Tastier Yet Smaller Meals? – Calorie Consumption and Willingness to Trade Food Quantity for Food Taste in Fast Food Products," *Marketing* 33, no. 4 (March 2011): 305–16, https://doi.org/10.15358/0344-1369-2011-4-305.

9 Thomas N. Robinson, Dina L.G. Borzekowski, Donna M. Matheson, and Helena C. Kraemer, "Effects of Fast Food Branding on Young Children's Taste Preferences," *JAMA* 298, no. 14 (2007): 1618.
10 Keith Spiller, "It Tastes Better Because … Consumer Understandings of UK Farmers' Market Food," *Appetite* 59 (April 2012): 100–7, https://doi.org/10.1016/j.appet.2012.04.007.
11 Jon May, "'A Little Taste of Something More Exotic': The Imaginative Geographies of Everyday Life," *Geography* 81, no. 1 (January 1996): 57–64, https://doi.org/10.1080/20436564.1996.12452531.
12 J. Nasser, "Taste, Food Intake and Obesity," *Obesity Reviews* 2, no. 4 (November 2001): 213–18, https://doi.org/10.1046/j.1467-789X.2001.00039.x.
13 Nasser, "Taste, Food Intake and Obesity," 216.
14 Nasser, "Taste, Food Intake and Obesity," 216.
15 Elisa Giampietri, Dieter B.A. Koemle, Xiaohua Yu, and Adele Finco, "Consumers' Sense of Farmers' Markets: Tasting Sustainability or Just Purchasing Food?" *Sustainability* 8, no. 11 (November 2016): 1157, http://doi.org/10.3390/su8111157; Ga-Eun (Grace) Oh and Anirban Mukhopadhyay, "Choice and Quantity in Conflict: Post-Taste Food Consumption and Inferences of Self-Control," *Advances in Consumer Research* 44 (2016): 274–8, https://hdl.handle.net/1783.1/84391.
16 Svetlana Bialkova, Lena Sasse, and Anna Fenko, "The Role of Nutrition Labels and Advertising Claims in Altering Consumers' Evaluation and Choice," *Appetite* 96 (January 2016): 38–46, https://doi.org/10.1016/j.appet.2015.08.030.
17 Yangjun Tu, Zhi Yang, and Chaoqun Ma, "The Taste of Plate: How the Spiciness of Food is Affected by the Color of the Plate Used to Serve It," *Journal of Sensory Studies* 31, no. 1 (February): 50–60, https://doi.org/10.1111/joss.12190.
18 Spiller, "It Tastes Better," 101.
19 Spiller, "It Tastes Better," 101.
20 Megan E. Waldrop and Carolyn F. Ross, "Sweetener Blend Optimization by Using Mixture Design Methodology and the Electronic Tongue," *Journal of Food Science* 79, no. 9 (September 2014), S1782–94, https://doi.org/10.1111/1750-3841.12575.
21 Lindsay Stringfellow, Andrew MacLaren, Mairi Maclean, and Kevin O'Gorman, "Conceptualizing Taste: Food, Culture and Celebrities," *Tourism Management* 37 (August 2013): 77–85, https://doi.org/10.1016/j.tourman.2012.12.016.
22 Lauren Gravitz, "Food Science: Taste Bud Hackers," *Nature* 486, no. 7403 (2012): S14–15, https://doi.org/10.1038/486S14a.
23 Allan Woods, "Is Poutine Canada's National Treasure or Culinary Appropriation?: Canadian Myths," *Toronto Star*, June 23, 2017, https://www.thestar.com/news/canada/is-poutine-canada-s-national-treasure-or-culinary-appropriation-canadian-myths/article_f6fffe2c-2cfb-5e25-9f04-d948623a99c4.html.
24 Woods, "Is Poutine Canada's National Treasure?"

5. With Poutine, History Matters

1 Mark Padoongpatt, "Sitting at the Table: Food History as American History," *American History* 103, no. 3 (December 2016): 686, https://doi.org/10.1093/jahist/jaw331.
2 Padoongpatt, "Sitting at the Table."
3 UFCW Canada, "By the Numbers: Canada's Food Service Industry." Media & News, https://www.ufcw.ca/index.php?option=com_content&view=article&id=31416:by-the-numbers-canada-s-food-service-industry&catid=9830&Itemid=6&lang=en.
4 Alain Girard and Pierre Sercia, "Immigration and Food Insecurity: Social and Nutritional Issues for Recent Immigrants in Montreal, Canada," *International Journal of Migration, Health and Social Care* 9, no. 1 (2013): 32–45, https://doi.org/10.1108/17479891311318566.
5 Girard and Sercia, "Immigration and Food Insecurity"; Immigration, Refugees and Citizenship Canada, "Canada Welcomes Historic Number of Newcomers in 2022," Government of Canada, January 3, 2023, https://www.canada.ca/en/immigration-refugees-citizenship/news/2022/12/canada-welcomes-historic-number-of-newcomers-in-2022.html.
6 "Get Your Greens in This Poutine," *Toronto Star*, January 22, 2019, E6.
7 "The Canadian Charter of Rights and Freedoms," Government of Canada, last modified April 16, 2025, https://www.justice.gc.ca/eng/csj-sjc/rfc-dlc/ccrf-ccdl/.
8 Stuart G. Nicholls and Patrick Fafard, "Genetic Discrimination Legislation in Canada: Moving from Rhetoric to Real Debate," *CMAJ: Canadian Medical Association Journal* 188, no. 11 (August 9, 2016): 788–9, https://doi.org/10.1503/cmaj.151170.
9 Jaakko Kauko and Anna Medvedeva, "Internationalisation as Marketization? Tuition Fees for International Students in Finland," *Research in Comparative and International Education* 11, no. 1 (March 2016): 98–114, https://doi.org/10.1177/1745499916631061.
10 Sandro Contenta, "Distinct? Let Me Count the Ways It's Not Just a Constitutional Hot Potato. Quebecers Are Unique in Their Culture, Language, History and, Yes, Politics," *Toronto Star*, March 24, 1996, F1.
11 Irene Bloemraad, "'Two Peas in a Pod,' 'Apples and Oranges,' and Other Food Metaphors: Comparing Canada and the United States," *American Behavioral Scientist* 55, no. 9 (2011): 1131–59, https://doi.org/10.1177/0002764211407844.
12 Lily M. Cho, "Mass Capture Against Memory: Chinese Head Tax Certificates and the Making of Noncitizens," *Citizenship Studies* 22, no. 4 (2018): 381–400, https://doi.org/10.1080/13621025.2018.1462505.
13 Bloemraad, "'Two Peas in a Pod,'" 1131–59.
14 The Quiet Revolution took place in Canada between the late 1950s and late 1960s. This era saw economic and social development in Quebec and Canada. This included rural electrification and health care initiatives.

15 Nicole Gombay, "Shifting Identities in a Shifting World: Food, Place, Community, and the Politics of Scale in an Inuit Settlement," *Environment and Planning D: Society and Space* 23, no. 3 (June 2005): 415–33, https://doi.org/10.1068/d3204.

16 Marcel Streng, "The Food Riot Revisited: New Dimensions in the History of 'Contentious Food Politics' in Germany Before the First World War," *European Review of History* 20, no. 6 (2013): 1073–91, https://doi.org/10.1080/13507486.2013.852517.

17 Stephanie Ketterer Hobbis, "'The Comic and the Rule' in *Pastagate*: Food, Humor and the Politics of Language in Quebec," *Food, Culture & Society* 20, no. 4 (2017): 709–27, https://doi.org/10.1080/15528014.2017.1357953.

18 Léon Dion and Micheline De Sève, "Quebec: Interest Groups and the Search for an Alternative Political System," *Annals of the American Academy of Political and Social Science* 413, no. 1 (May 1974): 124–44, https://doi.org/10.1177/000271627441300110.

19 Cheryl Gosselin, "Remaking Waves: The Québec Women's Movement in the 1950s and 1960s," *Canadian Woman Studies* 25, no. 3/4 (2006): 34–9; Michael Behiels, *Prelude to Quebec's Quiet Revolution: Liberalism vs Neo-Nationalism, 1945–60* (McGill-Queen's University Press, 1985).

20 Hubert Rioux Ouimet, "Quebec and Canadian Fiscal Federalism: From Tremblay to Séguin and Beyond," *Canadian Journal of Political Science* 47, no. 1 (March 2014): 47–69, https://doi.org/10.1017/S0008423914000237.

21 Hélène Vézina, Danielle Gauvreau, and Alain Gagnon, "Socioeconomic Fertility Differentials in a Late Transition Setting: A Micro-Level Analysis of the Saguenay Region in Quebec," *Demographic Research* 30, no. 1 (April 2014): 1097–128, https://doi.org/10.4054/DemRes.2014.30.38.

22 Emily Laxer and Anna C. Korteweg, "Party Competition and the Production of Nationhood in the Immigration Context: Particularizing the Universal for Political Gain in France and Québec," *Ethnic and Racial Studies* 41, no. 11 (2018): 1915–33, https://doi.org/10.1080/01419870.2017.1324168.

23 Arndt Leininger and Lea Heyne, "How Representative Are Referendums? Evidence from 20 Years of Swiss Referendums," *Electoral Studies* 48 (August 2017): 84–97, https://doi.org/10.1016/j.electstud.2017.05.006.

6. Cooking, Religions, and History

1 Abla Hasan, "Arab Cooking on a Prairie Homestead and Recollections from a Syrian Pioneer," *Great Plains Quarterly* 38, no. 4 (Fall 2018): 437, https://doi.org/10.1353/gpq.2018.0068; Grace O'Sullivan, Clare Hocking, and Valerie Wright-St. Clair, "History in the Making: Older Canadian Women's Food-Related Practices," *Food and Foodways* 16, no. 1 (2008): 63–87, https://doi.org/10.1080/07409710701885150.

2 Theodore Zeldin, "History of Cooking," *New Statesman* 89, no. 2287 (January 17, 1975): 86.

3 Anastasios Panagiotopoulos, "The Cooking of History. How Not to Study Afro-Cuban Religion by Palmié, Stephan," *Social Anthropology* 22, no. 1 (February 2014): 136–7, https://doi.org/10.1111/1469-8676.12065_14.

4 Rachel Laudan, *Cuisine and Empire: Cooking in World History* (University of California Press, 2015).

5 Marcel Detienne and Jean-Pierre Vernant, *The Cuisine of Sacrifice Among the Greeks* (University of Chicago Press, 1989).

6 Jonathan Lipnick, "Where Did Jesus Eat the Last Supper?" Israel Institute of Biblical Studies, September 7, 2016, https://blog.israelbiblicalstudies.com/holy-land-studies/where-did-jesus-eat-the-last-supper/.

7 Lipnick, "Where Did Jesus Eat the Last Supper?"

8 Stuart Strange, "The Cooking of History: How Not to Study Afro-Cuban Religion," *Comparative Studies in Society and History* 57, no. 1 (January 2015): 274–5, https://doi.org/10.1017/S001041751400067X.

9 Serge Gaudreau, "L'industrie du textile à Magog au XIXe siècle en textes et en images," *Journal of Eastern Townships Studies*, no. 18 (Spring 2001): 79.

10 Gail Cuthbert Brandt, "Women in the Quebec Cotton Industry, 1890–1950," *Material History Bulletin* 31 (Spring 1990): 99–105.

11 A.B. McCullough, review of *La production textile domestique an Québec, 1827–1941 : une approche quantitative et régionale* by Sophie-Laurence Iamoktagne, Fernand Harvey, *The Canadian Historical Review* 80, no. 1 (March 1999): 177–8, https://muse.jhu.edu/article/590507.

12 C. Bloskie, "Canada's Textile and Clothing Industries," *Canadian Economic Observer* 18, no. 3 (March 2005): 3.11–3.16.

13 Demet Uzuner and Belkiz Tarhan, *An Interdisciplinary Approach in Understanding Internet as a Practice: A Case Study of Internet Cafes in a Small Town* (MA thesis, Middle East Technical University, 2005).

14 Carrie Yodanis, "A Place in Town: Doing Class in a Coffee Shop," *Journal of Contemporary Ethnography* 35, no. 3 (June 2006): 341–66, https://doi.org/10.1177/0891241606286818.

15 Douglas McGray, "A Revolution in School Lunches. Getting Kids to Want to Eat Healthy Food Isn't Easy. Serving Wholesome Fare at Fast-Food Prices Is Even Harder. How Revolution Foods Is Helping School Cafeterias Swear Off Frozen Pizza and Fries," *Time* 175, no. 16 (2010): 50–3.

16 John Komlos, "The New World's Contribution to Food Consumption During the Industrial Revolution," *The Journal of European Economic History* 27, no. 1 (1998): 67–82.

17 Phillip McCann, "Global Village or Global City? The (Urban) Communications Revolution and Education," *Paedagogica Historica* 39, no. 1 (2003): 165–78, https://doi.org/10.1080/00309230307463.

18 Maher Said, Divyakant Tahlyan, Amanda Stathopoulos, Hani Mahmassani, Joan Walker, and Susan Shaheen, "In-Person, Pick Up or Delivery? Evolving Patterns of Household Spending Behavior Through the Early Reopening Phase of the COVID-19 Pandemic," *Travel Behaviour and Society* 31 (April 2023): 295–311, https://doi.org/10.1016/j.tbs.2023.01.003.

19 Lauren C. Ponisio and Paul R. Ehrlich, "Diversification, Yield and a New Agricultural Revolution: Problems and Prospects," *Sustainability* 8, no. 11 (November 2016): 1118, https://doi.org/10.3390/su8111118.
20 Sylvain Charlebois, "Opinion: Is the Kitchen Stove the Next Sewing Machine?" *London Free Press*, August 12, 2019, https://lfpress.com/opinion/columnists/opinion-is-the-kitchen-stove-the-next-sewing-machine.
21 Allison Harness, "What They Got: Condos," *Toronto Star*, April 18, 2015, H12.
22 Charlebois, "Opinion."
23 Charlebois, "Opinion."
24 VirtualFranchisee, "Cloud Kitchen Based Food Delivery: Business Plan," OGS Capital, January 2020, https://www.ogscapital.com/wp-content/uploads/2022/07/innovatorvisauk.pdf.
25 Charlebois, "Opinion."
26 David Marino-Nachison, "Food & Dining: Predicting the 'Death of the Kitchen,'" *Barron's*, June 20, 2018, https://www.barrons.com/articles/food-dining-predicting-the-death-of-the-kitchen-1529494200.
27 Charlebois, "Opinion."
28 "Dark Kitchens/Amazon: Fare Comment," *Financial Times*, May 17, 2019, https://www.ft.com/content/08197e4e-789f-11e9-bbad-7c18c0ea0201.
29 S. Akilimalissiga, N. Sukdeo, and A. Vermeulen, "The Delivery of Service Quality to Increase Customer Repurchase Behaviour and Customer Satisfaction at Fast Food Outlets in Central Johannesburg, South Africa," in *2017 IEEE International Conference on Industrial Engineering and Engineering Management (IEEM)* (IEEE, 2017), https://doi.org/10.1109/IEEM.2017.8290206.
30 Sylvain Charlebois, "Is the Kitchen Stove the Next Sewing Machine?" *AIMS*, August 19, 2019, https://www.aims.ca/op-ed/is-the-kitchen-stove-the-next-sewing-machine/.
31 Romain Cadario, "The Impact of Health Claims and Food Deprivation Levels on Health Risk Perceptions of Fast-Food Restaurants," *Social Science & Medicine* 149 (January 2016): 130–4, https://doi.org/10.1016/j.socscimed.2015.12.016.
32 Barry M. Popkin, "The Public Health Implications of Fast-Food Menu Labeling," *American Journal of Preventive Medicine* 43, no. 5 (November 2012): 569–70, https://doi.org/10.1016/j.amepre.2012.08.006.
33 Arun V. Mohan, Danny Mccormick, Steffie Woolhandler, David U. Himmelstein, and J. Wesley Boyd, "Life and Health Insurance Industry Investments in Fast Food," *American Journal of Public Health* 100, no. 6 (June 2010): 1029–30, https://doi.org/10.2105/AJPH.2009.178020.
34 Devajit Mohajan and Haradhan Kumar Mohajan, "Obesity and Its Related Diseases: A New Escalating Alarming in Global Health," *Journal of Innovations in Medical Research* 2, no. 3 (March 2023): 12–23, https://doi.org/10.56397/JIMR/2023.03.04.
35 Claire Thompson, Ruth Ponsford, Daniel Lewis, and Steven Cummins, "Fast-Food, Everyday Life and Health: A Qualitative Study of 'Chicken

Shops' in East London," *Appetite* 128 (2018): 7–13, https://doi.org/10.1016/j.appet.2018.05.136.

36 Claire Thompson, Ruth Ponsford, Daniel Lewis, et al., "Fast Food, Everyday Life."

37 Arun V. Mohan, Danny Mccormick, Steffie Woolhandler, et al., "Life and Health Insurance."

38 Donald S. Maier, "Should Biodiversity and Nature Have to Earn Their Keep? What It Really Means to Bring Environmental Goods into the Marketplace," *Ambio* 47, no. 4 (May 2018): 477–92, https://doi.org/10.1007/s13280-017-0996-5.

39 Gail Hamilton, "Eat This! How Fast-Food Marketing Gets You to Buy Junk (And How to Fight Back)," *CM: Canadian Review of Materials* 24, no. 31 (April 13, 2018): 1.

40 Jack Edmiston, "The Darkside of Poutine: Canada Taking Credit for Quebec Dish Amounts to Cultural Appropriation, Academic Says," *National Post*, May 28, 2017, https://nationalpost.com/news/canada/the-dark-side-of-poutine-canada-taking-credit-for-quebec-dish-amounts-to-cultural-appropriation-academic-says.

7. What Makes a Food Trend?

1 Sébastien LaRochelle-Côté, John Myles, and Garnett Picot, "Income Replacement Rates Among Canadian Seniors: The Effect of Widowhood and Divorce," *Canadian Public Policy* 38, no. 4 (December 2012): 471–95, https://doi.org/10.3138/CPP.38.4.471.

2 Jornt J. Mandemakers and Anne Roeters, "Fast or Slow Food? Explaining Trends in Food-Related Time in the Netherlands, 1975–2005," *Acta Sociologica* 58, no. 2 (May 2015): 123, https://www.jstor.org/stable/24569516.

3 Geci Karuri-Sebina, Karel-Herman Haegeman, and Apiwat Ratanawaraha, "Urban Futures: Anticipating a World of Cities," *Foresight* 18, no. 5 (2016): 449–53, https://doi.org/10.1108/FS-07-2016-0037.

4 Geci Karuri-Sebina, Karel-Herman Haegeman, and Apiwat Ratanawaraha, "Urban Futures."

5 Baojing Gu, Xiaoling Zhang, Xuemei Bai, Bojie Fu, and Deli Chen, "Four Steps to Food Security for Swelling Cities," *Nature* 566, no. 7742 (2019): 31–3, https://doi.org/10.1038/d41586-019-00407-3.

6 Geci Karuri-Sebina, Karel-Herman Haegeman, and Apiwat Ratanawaraha, "Urban Futures."

7 Geci Karuri-Sebina, Karel-Herman Haegeman, and Apiwat Ratanawaraha, "Urban Futures."

8 D. Stead, "Sustainable Development and the Future of Cities," *Urban Studies* 37, no. 4 (2000): 816–17.

9 Anthony William, *Medical Medium Celery Juice: The Most Powerful Medicine of Our Time Healing Millions Worldwide* (Hay House, 2019).

10 Charlsie Agro and Roxanna Woloshyn, "Is the Celery Juice Craze Driving Up the Price at the Supermarket?," *CBC*, April 29, 2019, https://www.cbc.ca/news/business/celery-juice-craze-trend-marketplace-1.5113735.

11 Juliano Laran and Anthony Salerno, "Life-History Strategy, Food Choice, and Caloric Consumption," *Psychological Science* 24, no. 2 (February 2013): 167–73, https://doi.org/10.1177/0956797612450033.
12 Matt Garcia, "Setting the Table: Historians, Popular Writers, and Food History," *The Journal of American History* 103, no. 3 (December 2016): 656–78, https://doi.org/10.1093/jahist/jaw328.
13 Garcia, "Setting the Table."
14 Mark Padoongpatt, "Sitting at the Table: Food History as American History," *American History* 103, no. 3 (December 2016): 686, https://doi.org/10.1093/jahist/jaw331.
15 G. Di Vita, G. De Salvo, S. Bracco, G. Gulisano, and M. D'Amico, "Future Market of Pizza: Which Attributes Do They Matter?" *Agris On-line Papers in Economics and Infomatics* 8, no. 4 (2016): 59–71.
16 Luis Guerrero, Maria Dolors Guàrdia, Joan Xicola, et al., "Consumer-Driven Definition of Traditional Food Products and Innovation in Traditional Foods: A Qualitative Cross-Cultural Study," *Appetite* 51, no. 2 (April 2009): 345–54.
17 G. Di Vita, G. De Salvo, S. Bracco, et al., "Future Market of Pizza," 59–71.
18 G. Di Vita, G. De Salvo, S. Bracco, et al., "Future Market of Pizza," 59–71.
19 Sylvain Charlebois, "The Grocerant: How Smart Grocery Stores Are Becoming Hybrids," *The Conversation*, November 1, 2017, https://theconversation.com/the-grocerant-how-smart-grocery-stores-are-becoming-hybrids-86641.
20 Olivia Chaffee, Annie McGillivray, Lisa Duizer, and Carolyn F. Ross, "Identifying Elements of a Ready-to-Eat Meal Desired by Older Adults," *Food Research International* 157 (July 2022): 111353, https://doi.org/10.1016/j.foodres.2022.111353.
21 Sylvain Charlebois, "The Rise of the 'Grocerant,'" *AIMS*, November 1, 2017, https://www.aims.ca/beacon/the-rise-of-the-grocerant/.
22 Charlebois, "The Rise of the 'Grocerant."
23 M. Hartnet, "Franchising: How Safe Are These Things?," *Restaurant Business* 91, no. 5 (1992): 66.

8. Creators, Ambassadors, and Franchises

1 *Maclean's*, "7 Surprising Facts about Poutine," August 15, 2012, https://macleans.ca/society/life/7-surprising-facts-about-poutine/.
2 The Canadian Encyclopedia, "Poutine," last edited May 23, 2023, https://www.thecanadianencyclopedia.ca/en/article/history-of-poutine.
3 Don MacDonald, "Say Cheese: A Strange Quebec Mishmash Celebrates 40 Years [Poutine]," *Report on Business Magazine* 13, no. 12 (June 1997): 13.
4 Susan Sampson, "Goodbye, Mr. Poutine," *Toronto Star*, March 10, 2004, D04.
5 Canadian Encyclopedia, "Poutine."
6 Mark Cleveland, Michel Laroche, Frank Pons, and Rony Kastoun, "Acculturation and Consumption: Textures of Cultural Adaptation," *International Journal of Intercultural Relations* 33, no. 3 (May 2009): 196–212, https://doi.org/10.1016/j.ijintrel.2008.12.008.

7 John Greenwood, "How Do You Like the New Food Network, Eh? Let's Kick It Up North a Notch! Canada, US Deal," *National Post* (Index-Only), July 5, 2000, C1.
8 Kevin Bissett, "NB Museum Celebrates the Humble Spud; Potato World, in the French Fry Capital of the World, Honours Local Farmers," *Chronicle Herald*, September 20, 2014, E2.
9 Canadian Encyclopedia, "Poutine."
10 Canadian Encyclopedia, "Poutine."
11 Amanda Kline, "Iconic Montreal Poutine Spot La Banquise Has Been Sold," *CTV News*, November 14, 2023, https://www.ctvnews.ca/montreal/article/iconic-montreal-poutine-spot-la-banquise-has-been-sold/.
12 Élise Tastet, "La Banquise: The Montreal Institution on Rachel Street," *Tastet*, August 25, 2023, https://tastet.ca/en/reviews/la-banquise-montreal-poutine/.
13 *Anthony Bourdain: No Reservations*, season 2, episode 4, "Quebec," April 17, 2006.
14 Chris Knight, *One World Kitchen: The Cookbook* (TouchWood Editions, 2015).
15 Chris Nuttall-Smith, "Heritage Minute," *Toronto Life* 45, no. 11 (November 2011): 97–8.
16 "Great Small Towns for … Food," *Texas Monthly* 32, no. 9 (September 2004): 1.
17 Robin Esrock, *The Great Central Canada Bucket List: One-of-a-Kind Travel Experiences* (Dundurn, 2015).
18 Amelia Levin, "Poutine," *Foodservice Equipment & Supplies* 69, no. 11 (November 2016): 16.
19 Julie Goulet, Véronique Provencher, Marie-Ève Piché, et al., "Relationship Between Eating Behaviours and Food and Drink Consumption in Healthy Postmenopausal Women in a Real-Life Context," *British Journal of Nutrition* 100, no. 4 (October 2008): 910–17, https://doi.org/10.1017/S0007114508925459.
20 Sonia Verma, "The Sticky Mess of the Origins of Poutine," *Globe and Mail* (Index-Only), December 7, 2009, A3.
21 John Allemang, "How Quebec's Artery Clogger Became Haute Poutine," *Globe and Mail* (Index-Only), May 22, 2010, A3.
22 "Poutine Invented 40 Years Ago," *Toronto Star*, October 1, 1997, E7.
23 Jean-Yves Girard, "Squick Squick," *Chatelaine* 55, no. 8 (August 2014): 18.
24 Ameya Charnalia, "Hitchhiking Across Canada en Français," *Toronto Star*, August 23, 2018, A3.
25 Caroline Durand, review of *Maudite poutine! L'histoire approximative d'un plat populaire* by Charles-Alexandre Théorêt, avec la collaboration d'Ève Derome et de Raphaël Martin, *Cuizine* 1, no. 2 (2009), https://doi.org/10.7202/037862ar.
26 Lauren Pelley, "Poutine Inventions Offer New Wheys to Eat Your Curds," *Toronto Star*, February 2, 2015, E1; "No Trifling with This: Poutine Is 40 Years Old [Invented by Fernand Lachance in 1957]," *Gazette* (Index-Only), 1997, D3.
27 Sampson, "Goodbye, Mr. Poutine."

28 Alan Gordon, "Teaching Quebec: Why Quebec's History Matters to English Canada," *Canadian Issues* (2013): 47–50.
29 Marion Kane, "The War of the Curds; A Victor Is Revealed in the Long-Standing Battle to be Declared Creator of Quebec's Famed Poutine," *Toronto Star*, November 8, 2008, L3.
30 B. Coutu, Denis Chamberland, Érick Tessier, and Ricardo Larrivée, *La poutine de Drummondville (On est les meilleurs)* (Canadian Broadcasting Corporation, 2017).
31 Suman Roy and Brooke Ali, *From Pemmican to Poutine: A Journey Through Canada's Culinary History* (Key Pub. House, 2010).
32 Sylvain Charlebois, "Que l'inventeur de la poutine se lève !," *La Presse*, July 21, 2019, https://www.lapresse.ca/debats/opinions/201907/20/01-5234592-que-linventeur-de-la-poutine-se-leve-.php; Yvette d'Entremont, "A Poutine Pilgrimage: What One Professor Learned by Digging into the Origins of the Iconic Canadian Dish," *Toronto Star*, August 2, 2019, https://www.thestar.com/halifax/a-poutine-pilgrimage-what-one-professor-learned-by-digging-into-the-origins-of-the-iconic/article_ae17800c-77ff-58b1-8ab7-7db47386f952.html.
33 Liz Fleming, "Quebec City Snack Shops Have True Passion for Poutine; Weather Bargains Make Ashton's a Real Hot Spot When It's Cold Outside," *Toronto Star*, July 21, 2007, T10.
34 Andy Blatchford, "World Poutine-Eating Contest to be Held in Toronto. Yes, That's Right. TO," *Canadian Press*, April 15, 2010.
35 Jessica Murphy, "Quebec Poutine Festival Confirms Working-Class Dish Now Haute Cuisine," *Canadian Press*, August 31, 2008, 1.
36 Canadian Encyclopedia, "Poutine."
37 G. Pierre Goad, "In the US, They'll Probably Try Renaming It McGlop or Big Muck," *Wall Street Journal*, March 8, 1990, B1.
38 Davida Aronovitch, "Poutine," *Britannica*, August 22, 2024, https://www.britannica.com/topic/poutine#ref1231601.
39 "Smoke's Poutinerie Gravy Plane Lands Its First Mobile Eatery at Toronto Pearson International Airport," *Canada NewsWire*, February 9, 2018, https://www.newswire.ca/news-releases/smokes-poutinerie-gravy-plane-lands-its-first-mobile-eatery-at-toronto-pearson-international-airport-673562313.html.
40 Lisa Jennings, "Smoke's Poutinerie Plans US Expansion," *Nation's Restaurant News*, June 12, 2015, https://www.nrn.com/food-trends/smoke-s-poutinerie-plans-us-expansion.
41 Corey Mintz, "Les périls de vendre de la poutine au Qatar," *L'Actualité* 44, no. 6 (June 2019): 42–5.
42 Sarah Barmak, "There Will Be Gravy,*" *Canadian Business* 89, nos. 7/8 (Summer): 74–80.
43 Etan Vlessing, "Meet Ryan Smolkin, Toronto's King of Poutine," *Hollywood Reporter*, September 7, 2017, https://www.hollywoodreporter.com/lifestyle/lifestyle-news/meet-ryan-smolkin-torontos-king-poutine-1034804/.
44 Blatchford, "World Poutine-Eating Contest."

45 Jennifer Allford, "Every Day Is a Snow Day at Quebec City's Carnaval," *Toronto Star*, September 2, 2017, T.7.
46 Fleming, "Quebec City Snack Shops."
47 Sonia Reid, *Ashton Leblond: Juste du vrai ! : Un rêve réalisé … une frite à la fois ! (Collection Autrement dit)* (Le Dauphin blanc, 2017).
48 Fleming, "Quebec City Snack Shops."
49 "Poutine Québécois," *Cook's Info*.
50 Nicole Allard, "Hector Berthelot, 1842–1895, et la caricature dans la petite presse satirique au Québec entre 1860 et 1895" (MA thesis, Université Laval, 1997).
51 Roy and Ali, *From Pemmican to Poutine*.
52 "Poutine," Merriam-Webster, accessed May 12, 2025, https://www.merriam-webster.com/dictionary/poutine.
53 Marie-Eve Dubois, "Le grand Larousse gastronomique," *Actualité Médicale* 28, no. 40 (2007): 43.
54 Yaakov Hoffman, Oded Bein, and Anat Maril, "Explicit Memory for Unattended Words: The Importance of Being in the 'No.'" *Psychological Science* 22, no. 12 (December 2011): 1490–3, https://doi.org/10.1177/0956797611419674.
55 Gusztáv Morvai and Benjamin Weiss, "Universal Tests for Memory Words," *IEEE Transactions on Information Theory* 59, no. 10 (October 2013): 6873–9, https://doi.org/10.1109/TIT.2013.2268913.
56 Markus J. Hofmann, Lars Kuchinke, Chris Biemann, Sascha Tamm, and Arthur M. Jacobs, "Remembering Words in Context as Predicted by an Associative Read-Out Model," *Frontiers in Psychology* 2 (2011): 252, https://doi.org/10.3389/fpsyg.2011.00252.
57 Stephen R. Schmidt, "Memory for Emotional Words in Sentences: The Importance of Emotional Contrast," *Cognition & Emotion* 26, no. 6 (2012): 1015–35, https://doi.org/10.1080/02699931.2011.631986.
58 Antonia Kronlund and Bruce W.A. Whittlesea, "Remembering Words and Brands After a Perception of Discrepancy," *Advances in Consumer Research* 35 (2008): 1.
59 "La poutine, une tradition de Cagnes … en France!," *Gravel le matin avec Alain Gravel, Radio-Canada*, April 2, 2019, https://ici.radio-canada.ca/premiere/emissions/gravel-le-matin/segments/chronique/112366/hugo-lavoie-poutine-peche-cagnes-sur-mer.
60 Kelly Robart, "It's All Relative," *Saltscapes*, n.d., https://www.saltscapes.com/kitchen-party/1771-its-all-relative.html.
61 Diane Carmel Léger and Tamara Thiebaux-Heikalo, *La patate cadeau ou La "vraie" histoire de la poutine râpée* (Bouton d'or Acadie, 2014).

9. Poutine: Canada's Pizza

1 Nattida Chotechuang, "Taste Active Components in Thai Foods: A Review of Thai Traditional Seasonings," *Nutrition & Food Sciences* 1, Suppl 10 (2013): 1–7, https://doi.org/10.4172/2155-9600.S10-004.

2 ET Bureau, "Culinary Identity: What Makes a Dish Attain National Status? [Panache]," *The Economic Times*, April 27, 2015.
3 Donna Gabaccia, *We Are What We Eat: Ethnic Foods and the Making of Americans* (Harvard University Press, 2000).
4 Tracie McMillan, *The American Way of Eating: Undercover at WalMart, Applebees, Farm Fields and the Dinner Table* (Scribners, 2012).
5 Michael P. Marino and Margaret S. Crocco, "Pizza: Teaching US History Through Food and Place," *The Social Studies* 106, no. 4 (May 2015): 149–58.
6 Zachary Nowak, "Folklore, Fakelore, History," *Food, Culture & Society* 17, no. 1 (2014): 103–24, https://doi.org/10.2752/175174414X13828682779249.
7 Hasia Diner, *Hungering for America: Italian, Irish and Jewish Foodways in the Age of Migration* (Harvard University Press, 2001).
8 Marino and Crocco, "Pizza," 1–10.
9 Food companies in rural Canada are not uncommon. Most iconic businesses in food are operated in small towns. Maple Leaf and McCain are companies that have achieved success by starting their businesses in small towns where they were close to their commodities. So it makes sense that McCain is located in Florenceville, New Brunswick. New Brunswick is acknowledged as an international leader in potato production. Interestingly, Florenceville is a small town with a population of roughly 1,500 people. Today, they have a museum that celebrates the company and the farmers it works with. I visited the museum and found it quite interesting.
10 Peter Genovese, *Pizza City: The Ultimate Guide to New York's Favorite Food* (Rutgers University Press, 2013).
11 Roger Collier, "Competitive Consumption: A Profusion of Pie, Pizza and Pulled Pork," *CMAJ: Canadian Medical Association Journal* 185, no. 4 (March 5, 2013): 290–1, https://doi.org/10.1503/cmaj.109-4394.
12 Natacha Chevalier, "Iconic Dishes, Culture and Identity: The Christmas Pudding and Its Hundred Years' Journey in the USA, Australia, New Zealand and India," *Food, Culture & Society* 21, no. 3 (2018): 367–83, https://doi.org/10.1080/15528014.2018.1451042.
13 Scott Baxter, "5 Iconic Wimbledon Food and Drinks," *Play Your Court*, June 28, 2016, https://www.playyourcourt.com/news/improve/5-iconic-wimbledon-food-and-drinks/.
14 Peter Scholliers, *Food, Drink and Identity: Cooking, Eating and Drinking in Europe Since the Middle Ages* (Berg, 2001).
15 Stephen Mennell, *All Manners of Food: Eating and Taste in England and France from the Middle Ages to the Present* (B. Blackwell, 1985).
16 Kaori O'Connor, "The King's Christmas Pudding: Globalization, Recipes, and the Commodities of Empire," *Journal of Global History* 4, no. 1 (March 2009): 127–55, https://doi.org/10.1017/S1740022809002988.
17 O'Connor, "The King's Christmas Pudding."
18 David Beriss, "Red Beans and Rebuilding. An Iconic Dish, Memory and Culture in New Orleans," *Appetite* 56, no. 2 (April 2011): 520, https://doi.org/10.1016/j.appet.2010.11.164.
19 Benita Gingerella, "Keeping Iconic Dishes Up to Date," *Foodservice Director* 31, no. 12 (December 2018): 15.

20 Libby Platus, "Culture Splash," *Restaurant Hospitality* 95, no. 3 (March 2011): 34–6.
21 Leor M. Hackel, Géraldine Coppin, Michael J.A. Wohl, and Jay J. Van Bavel, "From Groups to Grits: Social Identity Shapes Evaluations of Food Pleasantness," *Journal of Experimental Social Psychology* 74 (January 2018): 270–80, https://doi.org/10.1016/j.jesp.2017.09.007.
22 Elke U. Weber and Michael W. Morris, "Culture and Judgment and Decision Making: The Constructivist Turn," *Perspectives on Psychological Science* 5, no. 4 (July 2010): 410–19, https://doi.org/10.1177/1745691610375556.
23 Tegan Cruwys, Michael J. Platow, Sarah A. Angullia, et al., "Modeling of Food Intake Is Moderated by Salient Psychological Group Membership," *Appetite* 58, no. 2 (April 2012): 754–7, https://doi.org/10.1016/j.appet.2011.12.002.
24 Leor M. Hackel, Géraldine Coppin, Michael J.A. Wohl, et al., "From Groups to Grits."
25 Chelsea Chuck, Samantha A. Fernandes, and Lauri L. Hyers, "Awakening to the Politics of Food: Politicized Diet as Social Identity," *Appetite* 107 (December 2016): 425–36, https://doi.org/10.1016/j.appet.2016.08.106.
26 Anthony J. McMichael, John W. Powles, Colin D. Butler, and Ricardo Uauy, "Food, Livestock Production, Energy, Climate Change, and Health," *The Lancet* 370, no. 9594 (October 6, 2007): 1253–63, https://doi.org/10.1016/S0140-6736(07)61256-2.
27 Kazutoshi Sasahara, "You Are What You Eat: A Social Media Study of Food Identity," *Journal of Computational Social Science* 2, no. 2 (July 2019): 103–17, https://doi.org/10.1007/s42001-019-00039-7.
28 Natalia Mamonova and Lee-Ann Sutherland, "Rural Gentrification in Russia: Renegotiating Identity, Alternative Food Production and Social Tensions in the Countryside," *Journal of Rural Studies* 42 (December 2015): 154–65, https://doi.org/10.1016/j.jrurstud.2015.10.008.
29 Annemette Nielsen and Lotte Holm, "Food Shopping and Weight Concern. Balancing Consumer and Body Normality," *Appetite* 82 (November 2014): 213–20, https://doi.org/10.1016/j.appet.2014.07.024.
30 Andrew Shipley, "Social Comparison and Prosocial Behavior: An Applied Study of Social Identity Theory in Community Food Drives," *Psychological Reports* 102, no. 2 (April 2008): 425–34, https://doi.org/10.2466/pr0.102.2.425-434.
31 Grace E. Coolidge, review of *At the First Table: Food and Social Identity in Early Modern Spain* by Jodi Campbell, *Renaissance Quarterly* 71, no. 2 (Summer 2018): 728–30, https://doi.org/10.1086/699078.
32 Simon Anholt, *Places: Identity, Image, and Reputation* (Palgrave Macmillan, 2010).
33 Tanja Passow, Rolf Fehlmann, and Heike Grahlow, "Country Reputation – From Measurement to Management: The Case of Liechtenstein," *Corporate Reputation Review* 7, no. 4 (January 2005): 309–26, https://doi.org/10.1057/palgrave.crr.1540229.
34 Wantanee Suntikul, "Gastrodiplomacy in Tourism," *Current Issues in Tourism* 22, no. 9 (2019): 1076–94, https://doi.org/10.1080/13683500.2017.1363723.

35 Janine Widler, "Nation Branding: With Pride Against Prejudice," *Place Branding and Public Diplomacy* 3, no. 2 (April 2008): 144–50, https://doi.org/10.1057/palgrave.pb.6000055.

36 Rhona Richman Kenneally, "The Cuisine of the Tundra," *Food, Culture & Society* 11, no. 3 (2008): 287–313, https://doi.org/10.2752/175174408X347874.

37 Jennifer J. Davis, "To Make a Revolutionary Cuisine: Gender and Politics in French Kitchens, 1789–1815," *Gender & History* 23, no. 2 (August 2011): 301–20, https://doi.org/10.1111/j.1468-0424.2011.01640.x.

38 Jack Yan, "Branding and the International Community," *Journal of Brand Management* 10, no. 6 (August 2003): 447–56, https://doi.org/10.1057/palgrave.bm.2540140.

39 Lorraine Brown, John Edwards, and Heather Hartwell, "A Taste of the Unfamiliar. Understanding the Meanings Attached to Food by International Postgraduate Students in England," *Appetite* 54, no. 1 (February 2010): 202–7, https://doi.org/10.1016/j.appet.2009.11.001.

40 Colin K. Khoury, Anne D. Bjorkman, Hannes Dempewolf, et al., "Increasing Homogeneity in Global Food Supplies and the Implications for Food Security," *Proceedings of the National Academy of Sciences of the United States of America* 111, no. 11 (March 18, 2014): 4001–6, https://doi.org/10.1073/pnas.1313490111.

41 Torben Hansen, Maria Ingerslev Sørensen, and Marie-Louise Riewerts Eriksen, "How the Interplay between Consumer Motivations and Values Influences Organic Food Identity and Behavior," *Food Policy* 74 (January 2018): 39–52, https://doi.org/10.1016/j.foodpol.2017.11.003.

42 David Bell and Gill Valentine, *Consuming Geographies: We Are Where We Eat* (Routledge, 1997).

43 Warren Belasco and Philip Scranton, eds., *Food Nations: Selling Tastes in Consumer Societies* (Routledge, 2002).

44 Wynne Wright and Alexis Annes, "Halal on the Menu?: Contested Food Politics and French Identity in Fast-Food," *Journal of Rural Studies* 32, no. C (October 2013): 388–99, https://doi.org/10.1016/j.jrurstud.2013.08.001.

45 Scholliers, *Food, Drink and Identity*.

46 Jessica M.C. Pearce-Duvet, Martin Moyano, Frederick R. Adler, and Donald H. Feener Jr., "Fast Food in Ant Communities: How Competing Species Find Resources," *Oecologia* 167, no. 1 (September 2011): 229–40, https://doi.org/10.1007/s00442-011-1982-4.

47 Andrea Ciliotta-Rubery, "Food Identity and Its Impact upon the Study Abroad Experience," *Journal of International Students* 6, no. 4 (October 2016): 1062–8, https://doi.org/10.32674/jis.v6i4.336.

48 Widler, "Nation Branding."

49 Alvin F. Sherman, Jr., "Food, War and National Identity in Almudena Grandes' Inés y la alegría," *Bulletin of Spanish Studies* 93, no. 2 (2016): 255–74, https://doi.org/10.1080/14753820.2014.985113.

50 Pamela Parseghian, "Armenia's Hospitality and Culinary Traditions Thrive in a Region with a Troubled History," *Nation's Restaurant News* 40, no. 43 (October 23, 2006): 26.

51 Joanna Barszewska Marshall, "'Boast Now, Chicken, Tomorrow You'll Be Stew': Pride, Shame, Food, and Hunger in the Memoirs of Esmeralda Santiago," *MELUS* 32, no. 4 (December 2007): 47–68, https://doi.org/10.1093/melus/32.4.47.
52 Srđan Šapić, Srđan Furtula, and Danijela Durkalić, "Prestige and National Identity as Predictors of Food Products Purchase," *Ekonomika Poljoprivrede* 65, no. 2 (2018): 643–57. https://doi.org/10.5937/ekoPolj1802643S.
53 Claudia Bell and Lindsay Neill, "A Vernacular Food Tradition and National Identity in New Zealand," *Food, Culture & Society* 17, no. 1 (2014): 49–64, https://doi.org/10.2752/175174414X13828682779122.

10. Is the Mighty Poutine …

1 Rebecca Nicholson, "Poutine: The Posh Chips and Gravy Taking Over the World," *The Guardian*, September 7, 2014, https://www.theguardian.com/lifeandstyle/shortcuts/2014/sep/07/poutine-the-posh-chips-and-gravy-taking-over-the-world.
2 Debra A. Zellner, Susan Loaiza, Zuleyma Gonzalez, et al., "Food Selection Changes Under Stress," *Physiology & Behavior* 87, no. 4 (April 2006): 789–93, https://doi.org/10.1016/j.physbeh.2006.01.014.
3 "Fragmented Food Habits: New Dal Study Explores How Canadians Eat," *Dal News*, May 19, 2017, www.dal.ca/news/2017/05/19/dal-study-explores-eating-habits-across-canada.html.
4 Brian Wansink, Matthew M. Cheney, and Nina Chan, "Exploring Comfort Food Preferences Across Age and Gender," *Psychology & Behavior* 79, nos. 4–5 (September 2003): 739–47, https://doi.org/10.1016/S0031-9384(03)00203-8.
5 Mike Fitzpatrick, "Junk Food," *The Lancet* 363, no. 9413 (March 20, 2004): 1000, https://doi.org/10.1016/S0140-6736(04)15815-7.
6 Wansink et al., "Exploring Comfort Food Preferences," 739–47.
7 Laurette Dubé, Jordan L. LeBel, and Ji Lu, "Affect Asymmetry and Comfort Food Consumption," *Physiology & Behavior* 86, no. 4 (November 2005): 559–67, https://doi.org/10.1016/j.physbeh.2005.08.023.
8 Jordan D. Troisi and Shira Gabriel. "Chicken Soup Really Is Good for the Soul: 'Comfort Food' Fulfills the Need to Belong," *Psychological Science* 22, no. 6 (June): 747–53, https://doi.org/10.1177/0956797611407931.
9 M.S. Tryon, Rashel DeCant, and K.D. Laugero, "Having Your Cake and Eating It Too: A Habit of Comfort Food May Link Chronic Social Stress Exposure and Acute Stress-Induced Cortisol Hyporesponsiveness," *Physiology & Behavior* 114–15 (April 2013): 32–7, https://doi.org/10.1016/j.physbeh.2013.02.018.
10 Stacy Wood, "The Comfort Food Fallacy: Avoiding Old Favorites in Times of Change," *Journal of Consumer Research* 36, no. 6 (April 2009): 950–63, https://doi.org/10.1086/644749.
11 Atsuko Hashimoto and David J. Telfer, "Selling Canadian Culinary Tourism: Branding the Global and the Regional Product," *Tourism Geographies* 8, no. 1 (2006): 31–55, https://doi.org/10.1080/14616680500392465.

12 Anne Soon Choi, "'La Choy Chinese Food Swings American?': Korean Immigrant Entrepreneurship and American Orientalism Before World War II," *Cultural and Social History* 13, no. 4 (2016): 521–38, https://doi.org/10.1080/14780038.2016.1200817.

13 Francis Snyder and Lili Ni, "Chinese Apples and the Emerging World Food Trade Order: Food Safety, International Trade, and Regulatory Collaboration between China and the European Union," *The Chinese Journal of Comparative Law* 5, no. 2 (October 2017): 253–307, https://doi.org/10.1093/cjcl/cxx014.

14 Robert Klara, "Perspective: Fast-Food Nation," *Adweek* 53, no. 10 (March 12–18, 2012): 44–5.

15 Lawrence Solomon, "New Immigrants Enrich Canadian Cities," *National Post* (Index-Only), February 7, 2004, FP11.

16 Janine Chi, "Consuming Rice, Branding the Nation," *Contexts* 13, no. 3 (Summer 2014): 50–5, https://doi.org/10.1177/1536504214545761.

17 M. Susan Caswell and Rhona M. Hanning, "Adolescent Perspectives of the Recreational Ice Hockey Food Environment and Influences on Eating Behaviour Revealed Through Photovoice," *Public Health Nutrition* 21, no. 7 (May 2018): 1255–65, https://doi.org/10.1017/S1368980018000289.

18 Habeeb Salloum, "The Taste of Tradition in Quebec," *Americas* 53, no. 2 (March 2001): 58–9.

19 Elianna Lev, "Classic Canadian Foods Everyone Needs to Try at Least Once," *Reader's Digest*, accessed May 5, 2025, https://www.readersdigest.ca/travel/canada/10-must-try-canadian-dishes/.

20 A gibelotte is a type of French stew made from rabbit or fish. The broth is made with white wine.

21 Lionel Laroche, "Manners Please: Are You Making the Right Impression with Your Prospective Clients Overseas? Social Behaviour Carries More Weight Than You Might Think," *Canadian Consulting Engineer* 40, no. 2 (March/April 1999): 49–54.

22 Margaret J. Wiener, "Island Cooking," *HAU: Journal of Ethnographic Theory* 5, no. 1 (Spring 2015): 535–40, https://doi.org/10.14318/hau5.1.029.

23 Guansheng Ma, "Food, Eating Behavior, and Culture in Chinese Society," *Journal of Ethnic Foods* 2, no. 4 (December 2015): 195–9, https://doi.org/10.1016/j.jef.2015.11.004; Waraphon Phimpraphai, Sirikachorn Tangkawattana, Suwicha Kasemsuwan, and Banchob Sripa, "Social Influence in Liver Fluke Transmission: Application of Social Network Analysis of Food Sharing in Thai Isaan Culture," *Advances in Parasitology* 101 (2018): 97–124, https://doi.org/10.1016/bs.apar.2018.05.004.

24 E. Franklin, "Magical Meals," *Scholastic Parent & Child* 17, no. 2 (2009): 51–2, 54, 58–9.

25 Mark Bittman, "Skewers and Sticks," *Restaurant Business* 90, no. 12 (1991): 201.

26 Karin Nordström, Christian Coff, Håkan Jönsson, Lennart Nordenfelt, and Ulf Görman, "Food and Health: Individual, Cultural, or Scientific Matters," *Genes & Nutrition* 8 (July 2013): 357–63, https://doi.org/10.1007/s12263-013-0336-8.

27 "Social Eating Connects Communities," University of Oxford, March 16, 2017, https://www.ox.ac.uk/news/2017-03-16-social-eating-connects-communities.

28 Ariel Rose Plotnick, *The Main Dish*, 2018, https://escholarship.org/uc/item/8b67t46n.

29 Juliana Melendrez-Ruiz, Stéphanie Chambaron, Quentin Buatois, Sandrine Monnery-Patris, and Gaëlle Arvisenet, "A Central Place for Meat, but What About Pulses? Studying French Consumers' Representations of Main Dish Structure, Using an Indirect Approach," *Food Research International* 123 (September 2019): 790–800, https://doi.org/10.1016/j.foodres.2019.06.004.

30 Caroline Dunn, K. Shelnutt, J. Karavolias, L. House, and A. Mathews, "Better Bundled: Combined Vegetable Side and Main Dish Items Increase Vegetable Consumption Among Elementary and Middle School Students," *Journal of Nutrition Education and Behavior* 48, no. 7 (Supplement) (July–August 2016): S15, https://doi.org/10.1016/j.jneb.2016.04.044.

31 David Marshall and Rick Bell, "Meal Construction: Exploring the Relationship Between Eating Occasion and Location," *Food Quality and Preference* 14, no. 1 (January 2003): 53–64, https://doi.org/10.1016/S0950-3293(02)00015-0.

32 Jean-Pierre Poulain, *Manger aujourd'hui: attitudes, normes et pratiques* (Privat, 2002).

33 Kilien Stengel and Jean-Jacques Boutaud, eds., *Cuisine du futur et alimentation de demain* (L'Harmattan, 2016).

34 Penelope J. Brockie and Andres V. Maricq, "In a Pickle: Is Cornichon Just Relish or Part of the Main Dish?" *Neuron* 68, no. 6 (December 22, 2010): 1017–19, https://doi.org/10.1016/j.neuron.2010.12.013.

35 Patricia Johanna Bulsing, Swetlana Gutjar, Nicolien Zijlstra, and Elizabeth H. Zandstra, "High Satiety Expectations of a First Course Promote Selection of Less Energy in a Main Course Picture Task," *Appetite* 87 (April 2015): 236–43, https://doi.org/10.1016/j.appet.2014.12.218.

36 William D. Chey, "Food: The Main Course to Wellness and Illness in Patients with Irritable Bowel Syndrome," *American Journal of Gastroenterology* 111, no. 3 (March 2016): 366–71, https://doi.org/10.1038/ajg.2016.12.

37 Penny Gordon-Larsen, David K. Guilkey, and Barry M. Popkin, "An Economic Analysis of Community-Level Fast Food Prices and Individual-Level Fast Food Intake: A Longitudinal Study," *Health and Place* 17, no. 6 (November 2011): 1235–41, https://doi.org/10.1016/j.healthplace.2011.07.011.

38 Douglas McGray, "A Revolution in School Lunches. Getting Kids to Want to Eat Healthy Food Isn't Easy. Serving Wholesome Fare at Fast-Food Prices Is Even Harder. How Revolution Foods Is Helping School Cafeterias Swear Off Frozen Pizza and Fries," *Time* 175, no. 16 (2010): 50–3.

39 Tatiana Andreyeva, Michael W. Long, and Kelly D. Brownell, "The Impact of Food Prices on Consumption: A Systematic Review of Research on the

Price Elasticity of Demand for Food," *American Journal of Public Health* 100 (February 2009): 216–22, https://doi.org/10.2105/AJPH.2008.151415.

40 Lisa M. Powell and Euna Han, "The Costs of Food at Home and away from Home and Consumption Patterns among US Adolescents," *Journal of Adolescent Health* 48, no. 1 (January): 20–6, https://doi.org/10.1016/j.jadohealth.2010.06.006.

41 Thomas Christian and Inas Rashad, "Trends in US Food Prices, 1950–2007," *Economics & Human Biology* 7, no. 1 (March 2009): 113–20, https://doi.org/10.1016/j.ehb.2008.10.002.

42 May A. Beydoun, Lisa M. Powell, Xiaoli Chen, and Youfa Wang, "Food Prices Are Associated with Dietary Quality, Fast Food Consumption, and Body Mass Index Among US Children and Adolescents," *The Journal of Nutrition* 141, no. 2 (February 2011): 304–11, https://doi.org/10.3945/jn.110.132613.

43 Martin J. Caraher, S. Lloyd, M. Mansfield, C. Alp, Z. Brewster, and J. Gresham. "Secondary School Pupils' Food Choices Around Schools in a London Borough: Fast Food and Walls of Crisps," *Appetite* 103 (August 2016): 208–20, https://doi.org/10.1016/j.appet.2016.04.016.

44 Karen Briere, "Canadians Believe Higher Food Prices on the Way: Survey." *The Western Producer*, May 16, 2025, https://www.producer.com/news/canadians-believe-higher-food-prices-on-the-way-survey/.

45 Philys Ogbemudia, "Smoke's Poutinerie Creates the Most Expensive Poutine in Canada," *Fresh Radio 104.5*, August 1, 2018, https://web.archive.org/web/20191206070104/https://1045freshradio.ca/news/4365166/smokes-poutinerie-creates-the-most-expensive-poutine-in-canada/.

46 Chad Cotti and Nathan Tefft, "Fast Food Prices, Obesity, and the Minimum Wage," *Economics and Human Biology* 11, no. 2 (March 2013): 134–47, https://doi.org/10.1016/j.ehb.2012.04.002.

11. Following the Poutine: A Pilgrimage

1 Lainesse was a smoker, a hard worker, and not overly educated. He was socially aware of his place when travelling. Little else is known about him. He passed away in 2015. "The Men Who Cooked Up a Classic: A Brainwave, Not Tradition, Produced Poutine, the Dish Quebeckers Love (or Hate) [Fernand Lachance & Eddy Lainesse]." *Globe and Mail* (Index-Only), 1997, A2.

2 "Menu: Poutines," Ashton, accessed May 5, 2025, https://chezashton.ca/les-frites-et-poutines/.

3 Liz Fleming, "Quebec City Snack Shops Have True Passion for Poutine; Weather Bargains Make Ashton's a Real Hot Spot When It's Cold Outside," *Toronto Star*, July 21, 2007, T10.

4 Diane Trembley, "Le roi de la poutine n'avait « plus le goût à la vie »," *Le Journal de Québec*, May 15, 2017, https://www.journaldequebec.com/2017/05/15/le-roi-de-la-poutine-navait-plus-le-gout-a-la-vie.

5 Sonia Reid, *Ashton Leblond: Juste du vrai ! : Un rêve réalisé … une frite à la fois ! (Collection Autrement dit)* (Le Dauphin blanc, 2017).

6 Barbara Hanratty, Beth Milton, Matthew Ashton, and Margaret Whitehead, "'McDonalds and KFC, It's Never Going to Happen': The Challenges of Working with Food Outlets to Tackle the Obesogenic Environment," *Journal of Public Health* 34, no. 4 (December 2012): 548–54, https://doi.org/10.1093/pubmed/fds036.
7 Reid, *Ashton Leblond.*
8 "Chez Ashton: des amoureux de la restauration rapide assurent la relève," *Devenir Entrepreneur*, last modified August 18, 2022, https://devenirentrepreneur.com/fr/articles/histoires-entrepreneurs/chez-ashton-amoureux-restauration-rapide-assurent-releve.
9 Lisa Tucker McElroy, "The Best Travel Finds of 2014," *Redbook* 222, no. 2 (February 2014): 116.
10 Charles Passy, "An Insider's Guide to Quebec City; Expert Advice on Where to Eat, Sleep, Play and Shop in the Capital of French-Speaking Canada," *Wall Street Journal*, March 3, 2016, www.wsj.com/articles/an-insiders-guide-to-quebec-city-1457038670.

12. Poutine Pilgrimage Continued around the World

1 "Iowa's Best Burger for 2019 Goes to New Restaurant," *Southwest Farm Press*, May 6, 2019, https://www.farmprogress.com/livestock/iowa-s-best-burger-for-2019-goes-to-new-restaurant.

13. The Future of Poutine

1 Pasquale E. Rummo, Katie A. Meyer, Annie Green Howard, James M. Shikany, David K. Guilkey, and Penny Gordon-Larsen, "Fast Food Price, Diet Behavior, and Cardiometabolic Health: Differential Associations by Neighborhood SES and Neighborhood Fast Food Restaurant Availability in the CARDIA Study," *Health and Place* 35 (September 2015): 128–35, https://doi.org/10.1016/j.healthplace.2015.06.010.
2 Joseph L. Graves Jr., "Great Is Their Sin: Biological Determinism in the Age of Genomics," *The Annals of the American Academy of Political and Social Science* 661, no. 1 (September 2015): 24–50, https://doi.org/10.1177/0002716215586558; Susan L. Prescott and Alan C. Logan, "Each Meal Matters in the Exposome: Biological and Community Considerations in Fast-Food-Socioeconomic Associations," *Economics and Human Biology* 27, pt. B (November 2017): 328–35, https://doi.org/10.1016/j.ehb.2017.09.004.
3 Lydia Martens, "Consuming Geographies: We Are Where We Eat," *Gender, Place and Culture* 5, no. 3 (November 1998): 316–18, https://www.proquest.com/docview/211169764.
4 Leonardo Casini, Caterina Contini, Caterina Romano, and Gabriele Scozzafava. "Trends in Food Consumptions: What Is Happening to Generation X?," *British Food Journal* 117, no. 2 (February 2015): 705–18, https://doi.org/10.1108/BFJ-10-2013-0283.

5 Mara Miele, "Creating Sustainability: The Social Construction of the Market for Organic Products" (PhD diss., Wageningen University, 2001).

6 Miele, "Creating Sustainability."

7 Joyce Slater and Adriana N. Mudryj, "Nurturing Future Generations: Household Food Practices of Canadian Children and Family Meal Participation," *Canadian Journal of Dietetic Practice and Research* 77, no. 3 (September 2016): 113–18, https://doi.org/10.3148/cjdpr-2015-050.

8 Junxiu Liu, Colin Rehm, Renata Micha, and Dariush Mozaffarian, "Trends in Quality and Quantity of Dietary Intake from Full-Service Restaurants and Fast Food Restaurants Among US Adults, 2003–2016 (P04-147-19)," *Current Developments in Nutrition* 3, no. S1 (June 2019): 352–5, https://doi.org/10.1093/cdn/nzz051.P04-147-19.

9 Jennifer Hoolachan, Kim McKee, Tom Moore, and Adriana Mihaela Soaita, "'Generation Rent' and the Ability to 'Settle Down': Economic and Geographical Variation in Young People's Housing Transitions," *Journal of Youth Studies* 20, no. 1 (2017): 63–78, https://doi.org/10.1080/13676261.2016.1184241.

10 Ilya Bañares, "Would You Live in a Condo Without an Oven? 162 Units in This Downtown Building Don't Have One," *Toronto Star*, June 10, 2019, https://www.thestar.com/news/gta/would-you-live-in-a-condo-without-an-oven-162-units-in-this-downtown-building/article_6167bc84-520e-5f77-a9bd-20e27534a61c.html.

11 Hyeon-Mo Jeon, Min-Jung Kim, and Hyun-Chul Jeong, "Influence of Smart Phone Food Delivery Apps' Service Quality on Emotional Response and App Reuse Intention – Focused on PAD Theory," *Culinary Science and Hospitality Research* 22, no. 2 (2016): 206–21, https://doi.org/10.20878/cshr.2016.22.2.017017.

12 "Is the Kitchen Dead?," *UBS Investment Bank*, June 18, 2018, https://web.archive.org/web/20200619234336/www.ubs.com/global/en/investment-bank/in-focus/2018/dead-kitchen.html.

13 Edward R. Sykes, Stephen Pentland, and Saverio Nardi, "Context-Aware Mobile Apps Using IBeacons: Towards Smarter Interactions," in *Proceedings of the 25th Annual International Conference on Computer Science and Software Engineering*, edited by Jordan Gould, Marin Litoiu, and Hanan Lutfiyya (IBM Corp, 2015).

14 Nora A. ALFaris, Jozaa Z. Al-Tamimi, Moneera O. Al-Jobair, and Naseem M. Al-Shwaiyat, "Trends of Fast Food Consumption Among Adolescent and Young Adult Saudi Girls Living in Riyadh," *Food & Nutrition Research* 59 (December 2015): 26488, https://doi.org/10.3402/fnr.v59.26488.

Index